LEARNING TO BE A
LEATHERMAN

D1282521

LEARNING TO BE A LEATHERMAN

— a rite of passage —

RODERICK W. CORRELL

Learning to be a Leatherman: A Rite of Passage
Copyright © 2022 by Roderick W. Correll

This is a memoir. It reflects the author's present recollections of experiences over a period of years. Certain names, locations, and identifying characteristics have been changed, and certain individuals are composites. Dialogue and events have been recreated from memory and, in some cases, have been compressed to convey the substance of what was said or what occurred.

All rights reserved. No part of this book may be used or reproduced in any form, electronic or mechanical, including photocopying, recording, or scanning into any information storage and retrieval system, without written permission from the author except in the case of brief quotation embodied in critical articles and reviews.

Book design by The Troy Book Makers
Printed in the United States of America
The Troy Book Makers • Troy, New York • thetroybookmakers.com

To order additional copies of this title,
contact your favorite local bookstore
or visit www.shoptbmbooks.com

ISBN: 978-1-61468-725-2

This book is dedicated to my wife, Chloe,
my heartthrob, helpmate and healer,
over the 72 years we have known and loved each other

CONTENTS

PREFACE

This is the story of a young man whose grandfather emigrated from Germany in 1893 and founded a leather merchandising business in New York City. It is the story of his growing up in the shadows of a highly respected grandfather and gifted father. It follows him as he was groomed and then tapped to run the business after his father died. It is a story of a young man, blessed with the riches and privilege earned by his forebears and his battle to become his own man. It is the story of an older version of that same individual making sense and coming to a better understanding of the challenges of being a father. It is a story about me. I was born to be a leatherman. Like it or not, that was my destiny. The libretto of this opera seria, the meat of the stories in this book, is the training I went through to assume my father's mantle and become a successful leatherman. Presaging any respectable opera, an overture provides hints of its theme. The overture to my opera is my upbringing. Its Finale, Epilogue, synthesizes the lessons I learned, in living my life and writing this book.

OVERTURE

My Upbringing – 1935-1947

I came into this world, placenta previa, on Sunday, May 12, 1935. It was a Mother's Day and I was my parents' first-born child. My name, as registered on my birth certificate, was Roderick Correll Loewenstein, a name that was changed to Roderick Correll in proceedings held in Nassau County Court on November 30, 1942. My middle name, Wessel, my mother's maiden name, was added shortly thereafter. Since that time, I have been known as Roderick Wessel Correll, the name I use when signing any legal documents. Being a Correll rather than a Loewenstein no longer bothers me but there were times when I was growing up that I wondered why my father decided to change his surname. Did he think, working at our family's business, Hermann Loewenstein, that he could hide his Jewish roots? Myths exist about why he chose to change our surname. A deathbed letter from Dad's mother to her children supposedly exists. In it, Helene Correll, a journalist and noted doctor, no doubt aware and affected by discrimination, instructs her children to change their names, from Loewenstein to Correll. Or was it because my father, declared "yachtsman of the year" prior to seeking membership in it, was "blackballed" by the admissions committee of the prestigious Manhasset Bay Yacht Club? The reasons for this change in our family's surname were never adequately explained, leading, at least in my case, to a sense of shame and a tendency to hide this fact from others. This feeling has, at times, darkened my days but, thanks to my wife and to the serendipitous appearance of mentors at times when I needed them, I have survived, and thrived, as a leatherman and in other facets of my life.

My birth occurred at Doctors Hospital, located on East End Avenue in New York City. My mom's obstetrician was Dr. Fredrick C. Freed, a stately Tennessean who looked a lot like Colonel Sanders, the Kentucky Fried Chicken king. Uncle Freddy, as he was known to me and my siblings, helped give birth to three of the four of us and became a good family friend. He and his partner, "Bookie," were fixtures at Sunday lunch in our small Upper East Side apartment. That ended in late 1937, two years before my brother Stevie, my parents' third child, was born and Dad decided it was time to move to larger quarters, one of three moves I endured as I was growing up.

The next stop for the family was a home on Long Island's North Shore, in Great Neck. A new community, Kenilworth, located in the village of Kings Point, was being developed when Dad started looking for new digs. It was appealing to him for two reasons: a Long Island Rail Road train station with adequate parking, that provided an easy, rapid commute to his office in downtown Manhattan, and the proximity to water, Manhasset Bay, a playground for the yachtsman Dad hoped to become. For him, this quiet residential community was an ideal spot to raise his growing family. Not so incidentally, it had a yacht club, a place at which he harbored his first sailboat, Surabaya, and began his love affair with long-distance yacht racing. For my mother, it was a good place to integrate into life in America. The house was large and airy, our neighbors had young families and were social and friendly. And for us kids, well, there were fields to roam and play in, wild blueberries and asparagus to pick, a wonderful pool at the community yacht club and a gang of kids to horse around with.

It was here that I learned, in those early days, how to be an entrepreneur, in a way that would be frowned upon today. Dad smoked a lot, three packs of Lucky Strikes a day. Mom smoked as well, one pack a day. Her brand was Chesterfield. Dad decided that setting me up as a cigarette vendor would be a great way for me to earn an allowance and learn a business lesson. A little wooden bookshelf was purchased onto which I stacked packs of cigarettes taken from the cartons Mom bought with me at the Manhattan market nearby in Great Neck's "Old Village." She charged me the price she paid for the cartons that she bought and I turned around, selling my parents packs at the price they would have paid for a single pack if they bought it at our local drug store. I didn't get rich, but I loved keeping store and learned, by doing, the concept of retail versus wholesale pricing.

Things started to change when Mom's mom, Sophie Geronne, fled Germany before World War II and came to live with us. Her addition to our household was definitely a positive, for me, my sister Lenie and brother Stevie. We loved our Omi. She had time for us whereas Mom did not. Running a busy household and acting as a gracious hostess when Dad brought customers home for dinner was a full-time job for Mom. Eventually she buckled under the strain and started self-medicating with frequent nips of alcohol. Her drinking problem was not evident to me or my siblings. She never looked slobbered, but I do remember the time she spent a few weeks in what Dad called a sanatorium. And when Omi moved from our home to an apartment at the Colony House Hotel shortly thereafter, none of us caught on to the tension between Mom and Omi. Dad informed us that "Omi has told me she feels a bit cramped in her bedroom here. Mom and I found her a nice place at the Colony House Hotel, near the train station in the New Village. She will have more room there and a park and plenty of shops nearby. She can walk to get her New York Times at the station, shop for anything she needs and take a stroll in the park. She will be happy!" Perhaps I should have taken notice. I was nine at the time, but that explanation satisfied me. My mom and dad never argued, about anything, at least not within my earshot, throughout the 22 years I lived at home with them. Hard to believe? Bewildering, actually. When Dad informed me, in 1957, no more than six months after Chloe and I were married, that he was divorcing Mom and remarrying, I was taken completely by surprise.

After this awakening, I became more attentive to words and attuned to body language. Anxious to be more aware of people's feelings, I jumped at the chance to study individual and group behavior. This I did when I returned to Yale for an MBA degree in 1983. Doing so paid emotional dividends. Prior to then I was clueless. Things like Mom's four-week absence and Omi's move to the Colony House triggered no alarm bells for me. Now, they might have. Prior to her departure, Omi kept dinnertime conversations alive when Mom was not at table. She talked about the past, the wonders experienced "taking the cure" at Bad Worishofen back in Germany. She had opinions about the present, the raging war in Europe, and she cared about the future. She even wrote letters to the Times, disagreeing with editorials she had read.

When Omi was no longer at our table, I remember with pleasure, not angst or suspicion, the Sunday lunches we used to have with her at the Colony House. Those visits always started with sherry for the old folks in Omi's apartment, followed by a rather festive lunch in the hotel's dining room. For us kids, those lunches included not only food. Adorning the dining table were paper doilies, embossed with decorative patterns, little chads that we could liberate with our fork tines. Of the three of us, Lenie was the most dexterous, the proud winner, most of the time, of our doily derby, the recipient of a chocolate candy, presented by Omi.

Distracted by diversions like this, it is understandable that I failed to notice the cracks starting to appear in my parents' marriage. Life was good, but it was not always rosy for me. My parents had to pull me out of kindergarten in 1941 when I got bullied for speaking German, the language I was used to hearing and speaking at home. Another boo-boo occurred shortly thereafter, a freak accident at the Kenilworth Yacht Club where a race around the pool wound up badly. Scampering down a ladder instead of diving into the pool was certainly misguided, a poor decision that resulted in a spiral fracture of my ankle that put me in a wheelchair for six months. Not fun, but a lesson important to learn, a blow lessened by Miss Bresnahan, my immensely compassionate first-grade teacher at Buckley Country Day School.

The eight years at Buckley bring back nothing but happy memories. I did well academically, I played sports avidly and I made good friends, meaningful relationships that lasted for years after I went off to the Lawrenceville School. Things at home were going smoothly, or so it seemed, ruffled only slightly by our move to Broadlawn Harbor in 1946. The reasons for this move were multiple, understandable but, viewed in retrospect, somewhat impulsive.

Firstly, housing another child, my sister Judy, born in October of 1944, called for extra bedrooms, not just one but two, a nursery for Judy and a smallish bedroom for Bridie, her Irish nanny. Secondly was the price at which the property, part of the expansive Angie Booth estate, was being listed. Subdivision of this estate, purchased by a realtor named Jim Curry, had been approved and it was now being developed into a residential community, which Jim had christened Broadlawn Harbor. The manor house, situated on five acres of the former estate's 50-acre tract, was the first parcel Jim was offering to the public. The manor house, a large, colonnaded, Tara-like structure, was a real gem.

Other features of the property included a separate carriage house with living quarters located above a three-car garage, a decorative wading pool in the back yard, a large sloping field that led down to 150 feet of waterfront on Manhasset Bay. Plenty of space and magnificent views and amenities like a community pool and yacht club tucked into a slightly more protected section of Manhasset Bay. Dad liked bargains. His business was doing well. He had some extra cash and this home was a dream he apparently could not resist. Dad was a showman but not a Gatsby, nowhere near as rich or flashy. Keeping up with the Jones was not in his lexicon, but this particular property had a panache he could not resist.

And thirdly, since losing his Surabaya in the 1944 monster hurricane, Dad was eager to buy another yacht and moor it not far from his home. This he could do easily if we lived at 19 Harbour Road in Broadlawn Harbor. Less than a quarter mile away, at the new yacht club that was being built, he would have access to a dock and be entitled to a mooring, at the base of Harbour Road, that would eventually be serviced by a club launch.

That was it, the tipping point. Buy this home, the only one on Harbour Road, Broadlawn's main drag at the time, build a new sailboat or buy one that was already afloat and fleet afoot. Having maintained contact with Knutson Marina and Shipbuilders in Halesite in the Suffolk County town of Huntington, Dad started his search there. At this yard, where the Surabaya had spent its winters, Dad conferred with the owner, Tom Knutson, and opted to have this yard build him a boat, a Pilot 33 sloop. It wasn't as big as the Surabaya or as classy as the 56-foot white Alden yawl, Tomahawk, he bought a few years later, but it kept him happy and on the water. Seeing it built was half the fun, a family affair. During the year it took for her to be built, we drove to Knutson's every weekend and stopped in East Norwich at Rothman's for steaks on the way back home. They were delicious, as are my memories of their sizzle, smell and taste.

Our five years in Broadlawn Harbor were some of my family's happiest ones. When we moved to Plandome Manor, Mom and Dad had separate bedrooms, but in Broadlawn, they slept in an ultra-large bedroom in a king-size bed into which they invited us kids each Sunday morning. What fun we had shooting ping-pong balls at a statue of Elizabeth, Dad's oldest sister, Mom's nemesis, for reasons we only found out years later. A bronze bust of "Aunt Betty" had been crafted by one of her artist friends. Why Dad had it remains a mystery, but there it was, atop a large armoire at the foot of their bed, a target for us to shoot at. Ready, aim, fire and shouts of glee when one of our ping-pong balls hit the target. How delightful it must have been, especially for Mom, to have her children strike back at the woman who, myth has it, had told Dad to "ship her back" not long after I was born. True or false, this evidence of my parents' togetherness, fighting a common foe, is a happy memory for me.

Of equal, if not greater significance was that I met Dave Strite in Broadlawn Harbor. He became my closest friend during my teenage years and my mentor in many ways. It was Dave who was the ringmaster when my sibs, a small gang of other kids and I played capture the flag, kick the can and other games in the fields that still existed nearby. It was Dave who organized the softball games we played on our large expanse of lawn and encouraged me to slow pitch Bridie so that we could watch her scamper around the bases after she wacked the ball out of everyone's reach. Dave and I also shared a hobby. We built model planes out of balsa wood, some powered by tightly wound rubber bands, others by miniscule gas engines. To test fly them, we needed large open fields. With none available nearby, we set our sights on finding ways of getting to Hicksville, where we could fly our little beauties. There were lots of fields there, potato fields laid fallow, awaiting development into a community called Levittown. It didn't happen often, but we occasionally got rides. Besides Bridie, my parents employed a cook, a gardener and a chauffeur/butler/handyman named Leonard Jones. I remember this gentle, stately, soft-spoken black man with great fondness. It was Leonard who took Dave and me to Hicksville to fly planes and, in later years, me and Chloe to Roosevelt Raceway, on a date, prior to my getting a driver's license.

There were other pastimes Dave and I shared: fishing, clamming and sailing. We would go out in Dad's rowboat and fish for flounder. We caught plenty. We also caught tommy cots and eels, a delicacy Omi adored but nothing we cared to come home with. Most of all, though, it was learning how to sail that made summers so much fun. Dave had a Lightning and, later on Dad bought me my own little boat, a Blue Jay. Sailing in those boats gave me a chance to get a feel for the sea and an opportunity to mimic the maneuvers I watched Dad perform when he put his new Pilot 33 through its paces. I would never be the sailor he was but these little forays gave me a love for the sea and a chance to practice being at the helm without hearing Dad remark that I was steering a snake's course. That was important for me, learning from experience, not from him, what I was doing right and wrong.

In those Broadlawn years, Dave and I did all those things together, but there is one that stands out above all the others. It was through Dave that I met my wife. She was his girlfriend Jeanette's best friend, a willowy young lass named Chloe Louise Anderson. Chloe, as I too often share with people, was a substitute for the blind date they had arranged for me. And for that serendipitous switch, I can only thank my lucky stars. It was not love at first sight, for either Chloe or for me, but that meeting was without question of huge importance for both of us. We dated sporadically through prep school, got closer during our early college years and, after I gave her my Phi Gam pin at the end of my junior year, we symbolically closed ranks. My marriage proposal followed not more than eight months later. I smile remembering the circumstances. As we rode back to New Haven in my car after a Harvard-Yale football game in Cambridge, I took my eyes off the road, turned my head slightly in her direction, and asked her to marry me. I could not get down on bended knee and I did not take my foot off the gas, but when I popped the question, she said yes. And so, we got married the following year, on July 6, 1957, six weeks after we graduated from college. It has been a marriage, not without its challenges, that has lasted over 65 years.

One final move of my family of origin needs mention before I get on with the story. I'm going to tell you about learning to be a leatherman. It was our move, in 1953, to Plandome Manor. This village, one of several in Manhasset, a town just to the east of Great Neck, and the house we moved into on Bayview Road, found us next to the Grummans of fighter plane fame and the Phillipses, who made their money in insurance, I believe. We never set foot on either of their estates or met anyone in their families, but we were definitely in fast company now.

Dad moved us to a large and beautiful house on three and a half acres just before I went off to Yale. As was the case in Broadlawn, our home sat right on the waterfront, on Manhasset Bay, with a clear view this time directly north towards City Island. This house, formerly a ferry depot, I believe, was smaller and lacked the columns of our home in Broadlawn, but it had style and warmth. There was something magical about it, especially at Christmastime. I can still picture the floor-to-ceiling windows that looked over the bay and the 10-foot-high beautifully decorated fir tree that was always placed just in front of them. Screwed into the trunk of these trees was a set of graduated-length wrought-iron candle holders, each holding a real live candle.

These were lit nightly during the holiday season and tended to with care while the candles were burning. It was during this season that music wafted through the house. Singing, with accompaniment by a well-tuned piano, brought magic into that room. Besides untrained voices like mine, there were people with whom Dad and Lenie sang at the Manhasset Congregational Church, some of them professionals, some who had performed on the stage of the Metropolitan Opera, one in a leading role. The pianist was no slouch either. Jean Lawson was the music director at the church. Her husband, Roblee, was the choir director. The results were mesmerizing, beautiful harmonies, candlelit surroundings, good German wine and delicious cookies.

We spent five wonderful years there. Parties like these were not unusual. Guests—my parents' friends, dad's staff and customers, Lenie's buddies from Manhasset High School and, later on Chloe, who lived in Manhasset—were frequently at our dinner table. My roommates from Lawrenceville and Yale occasionally stayed with us overnight. And for me there was an added plus. I now lived less than three miles away from Chloe. Was our Plandome Manor epoch the Correll version of Camelot? Yes, perhaps it was, but this euphoria, unfortunately was not long-term. Shortly after I married Chloe and moved out, the fractures in my parents' union started to appear and things went bad quickly.

ACT 1: LEARNING THE ROPES

SCENE 1:

Summers in the Swamp – 1948-1951

While I was being formally educated and growing into a young adult, Dad was starting to groom me to become a leatherman. Beginning when I was 12 years old, I spent all but one of my summer and Christmas vacations learning how to be a successful one. Our family's leather business, founded by my grandfather Hermann in 1893, was a merchandising company that owned a tannery in Gloversville, New York, had leather manufactured to its specifications in several other mills and was a manufacturer's representative for a number of other leather companies. Its suppliers included tanneries in the United States and overseas in England, Scotland, France, Italy, Germany, Belgium and Japan. It was located in New York City and sold its leathers principally to women's shoe and handbag manufacturers, many of whom were based in the city. The three-floor brick building at 26 Ferry St. that housed its office, warehouse and showroom was located in the city's leather district, an area called the Swamp that lay in the shadow of City Hall. In its day, this four-block area was a bustling, vibrant community populated by the sales offices of most of America's major tanneries and a number of foreign ones. Today, these offices are closed, their occupants are long gone and the factories they once served are shuttered, victims to the reality that it is cheaper to tan leather and make products out of it overseas. Our lovely old building? Razed. And Ferry Street itself? Gone, built over, just a memory now, part of the footprint of Pace University's downtown campus.

There were some dark days later, but my vacation work stints at Hermann Loewenstein Inc. as a youth were happy ones. My dad and I drove in from Great Neck, picking up two of his top executives along the way. Traffic then was not an issue and the views of the city as we crossed the Triborough Bridge and cruised down the East River Drive were stunning.

So was the smile of the operator of our quaint little elevator as he closed its floor door, pulled shut the cabin's scissor gate and yanked on the chain that started us upward to our office on the third floor. Upon arrival, Dad and I parted company and I got down to the business of learning about leather.

Dad's employees, at least most of them, were welcoming and very willing to teach me how to correctly judge the quality of a skin and decide into which grade it should be placed. To get me started, they wheeled a production load, called a pack, to a sorting table located next to a big window. To sort skins properly, you need excellent lighting conditions. Doing so in natural sunlight is important, in north light if possible. The north wall in our warehouse had large windows stretching its length, ideal for sorting, so a long table had been built, right under the windows, providing room for three to four sorters to do their magic simultaneously.

That's exactly what it was for me as a kid, magic. Feeling, touching, smelling and seeing the great variety of the leathers in that warehouse was almost mind boggling. Tanning those hides and skins, as I learned later, could be a messy, smelly, quite dangerous business, but handling finished leathers is quite the opposite. It was, even in those early days, a sensual experience that got into my blood and has never left it. The lessons I learned were taught to me by men who knew their trade. They seemed to love it and took to heart the prospect of teaching me the terms and tricks of the trade. There were tactile things that they felt I needed to learn, like the touch and feel of a hide or skin. There was the precision of color matching I needed to understand and grasp. There was the challenge of picking a bunch of skins off a "horse" and flipping them deftly onto a table and the dexterity needed to roll a dozen skins into a neat bundle. And then, most important of all, I had to know how to sort. This lesson had to be learned if I ever hoped to be successful in the leather business. Dad's sorters were masters. They went out of their way to teach me the art and the science of proper grading and trimming of the skins I was being given to sort. Vacation after vacation, session after session sorting took center stage. It seemed to me that I'd never learn, but the day did come when I was awarded a smile and a pat on the back by Frank Seimetz, our warehouse manager, and with that pat of encouragement, I started gaining confidence. When I came to work full-time at HL years later, another person took over that role. Joe Vago, a Hungarian Jew who had once owned a tannery there, immigrated to the U.S. following Russia's invasion of his homeland. With our business growing, Dad needed help and when he learned that there might be some experienced Hungarian leatherworkers among the new immigrants, he acted quickly. By the time I finished my six months active duty in the Army, in mid 1958, HL had moved to its new home on W 34th St and Joe was working for us as a sorter. I learned so much from Joe. He was just the sort of mentor I needed, an authentic leatherman, candid with his critiques, patient but eager to show me how to become one myself.

Other chores and activities occasionally were added to the mix. The company sent swatch pads and swatch books to all its customers. Those swatches needed to be cut, collated and assembled, tasks which, with proper training, I was able to handle. I remember, however, how nervous I was the first time I operated the clicker cutter we used to cut them. In those days, before OSHA required safety guards, most clickers, ours included, did not have them.

Another offsite activity I dreamed up for myself was well received by my dad. On the electric jigsaw in our basement, I cut out plywood horseheads to mount on one end of the horses in our showroom. Each horse was devoted to one of the product lines Dad had created and had a skin of each of the colors in that particular line draped on it. These horses were stored under a long table on top of which he put "story boards." These he used to give context to the product lines and colors he was showing his customers. Each horse was on wheels and, as he started talking about a particular line, he pulled out the horse on which these skins were draped. Now with my horseheads poking out from under the table, pulling those horses out was easier and more ceremonial. What fun he had telling his customers that his son had provided him with heads for those horses. And how proud I was.

There were other ways and venues that Dad devised to help me learn the leather business. Those would come later as I finished up at Lawrenceville and worked my way through Yale. While not always appreciated at the time, most proved valuable. In his way, Dad prepared me for the challenges that lay ahead and I'm glad he did, because there were many of them.

SCENE 2

Exploring Other Options – 1951

Dad realized I would need, at some point, to explore other career options. Working for someone else during my summer vacation that year, doing something that had nothing to do with leather, would give me a chance to spread my wings, or so he told me. As I look back at the job I worked at in the summer of 1951, a two-month stint at a Phelps Dodge Copper Corp. facility in Maspeth, Long Island, questions arise. The office where I worked was, being polite, a backwater. There were gray metal desks, gray metal filing cabinets, gray metal cushion-less chairs and lots of IBM punch cards sitting on the floor in corrugated paper cartons. The mission of our group was to determine the safety records of the Phelps Dodge refining facilities, spread all around the world. The punch cards waiting to be processed all told stories of accidents that had happened at these fa-cilities. My job was to feed these cards into electric sorting machines that would separate them into groups by category, i.e., same accident type, same location, same time of day, etc., etc., etc., and when that task was completed, to put these sorted cards into separate boxes. The work wasn't exactly stimulating, but the people were nice. I can even remember my boss's name, Frank Lippe. A bit strange that I would remember his name, given the shortness of our relationship, but not so curious, given the im-pression the kind of sorting I was doing for him made on me.

Sorting skins is something I had started learning how to do in the Swamp. Sorting data was a whole different ball game. In future years, this awareness of how data sorting could help me solve problems and pay financial dividends developed into a passion for creating spreadsheets. Using what-if scenarios to help solve business problems first got my at-tention in 1967, after Dad died, when I was forced to come up with a reorganization plan for Hermann Loewenstein. The decisions facing me were critical and stressful. Closing our office, warehouse and showroom in New York City looked like it was the only way to make ends meet. This action, which meant closing our New York City HQ, moving and probably letting 30 people go, many of whom I had known and worked with for many years, was incredibly stressful. Realizing the bias many of Dad's executive team and some of our professional advisors had for staying the course, I looked outside for more objective perspectives. With the help of a friend who lived nearby in Cold Spring Harbor, I started building a what-if scenario, a spreadsheet that allowed me to weigh the options available to me. Moving numbers around on it did not eliminate the pain, but it helped me try to mitigate its effect on the people who would be affected, including me. Years later, in 1979, when it was first introduced, I learned about VisiCalc and realized how this program could help me rebuild my business. Compared to today's spreadsheets and database programs, VisiCalc was in the dark ages. Primitive or not, it was an eye opener that introduced me to a means of sorting and manipulating data. Allowing me to construct what-if scenarios that shed light on many of the challenges I faced, I was able to confront them and turn them into opportunities. Even today, in retirement, I find myself using spreadsheets when I want to analyze a problem and evaluate my options for solving it.

Was fanning a passion for spreadsheets in Dad's mind when he proposed that I go work in Maspeth for his friend Cart Harloff during the summer of 1951? Did he recognize the value that computers would eventually offer to decision makers? Was he at all concerned that my exposure to data sorting by machine would intrigue me to pursue a career in the computer industry? I doubt it. Somehow, I think that quite the opposite was true. My guess is that he felt a summer working for a large company, doing a mind-numbing task would convince me that working for him at Hermann Loewenstein was a far better option.

ACT 2: IN THE MILLS

SCENE 1:

Introduction to Tanning Across the Pond – 1952

This part of the story of my becoming a leatherman is about a trip that took place 70 years ago. It is anchored by vivid memories I retain about the people we met and the places we visited. Its accuracy is further aided by research I conducted on the internet and in conversations I had with some of the people I met who are still alive. I've reached out to others in hopes of finding documents and pictures that might ensure truthfulness and color to my tale. The search goes on, but I feel I now have in hand, head and heart, the data and feelings to tell you what it was like for me to take this trip.

Facts like weather conditions on a given day are, in large part, imagined. Distances between the way points on our bicycle trip are guesstimated, based on mileage on current roadways, as reported by Google. Quotes attributed to some of the people with whom we interacted are contextually accurate but not verbatim. And since ships' manifests remain to be found, the sailing dates of our two Atlantic passages remain a mystery. That said, let's move on to see how I spent that summer across the pond.

I'd learned how to handle and judge leather, working virtually all my vacations doing a variety of jobs at Hermann Loewenstein, our family's firm. It was now time, my dad decided, to introduce me to what it took to transform gucky, grungy rawhides into supple, attractive pieces of leather. In other words, learning what it takes to tan hides and skins. It was a bit too early for me to learn the chemistry involved, but Dad felt that getting down and dirty was a good idea. Actually, handling hides as they moved from process to process through the "wet end" of a tannery, that, he told me, would be a real eye, ear and nose opener. With this in mind, he crafted a plan, a two-month trip to the United Kingdom, together with my best friend Dave Strite. We would travel there and back by sea, spend two weeks working in a Scottish tannery and three weeks cycling through Scotland and England. "Combine business with pleasure whenever you can," he said. That was his mantra, a lesson I learned well and readily adopted,

For our work stint, Dad had settled on what he felt would be an ideal venue, the W. & J. Martin tannery, on Baltic Street in Glasgow, Scotland. W. & J. Martin transformed big, heavy Scottish ox, steer and heifer rawhides into rugged, long-lasting men's boot and shoe leather. The firm had a storied history. It was a pioneer in the development of chrome-tanned shoe leather, a process that, compared to its precursor, hides that were vegetable-tanned, dramatically reduced their absorbency and considerably reduced the time taken to produce them. Boots made out of the company's heavy-duty, chrome-tanned "Zug" played a significant role in World War I. Trench warfare characterized this conflict and when the vegetable-tanned boots issued to Black Jack Pershing's American troops started to rot and fall apart, something had to be done. The answer was boots made out of chrome-tanned leather like W&JM's Zug. These boots kept their feet dry. They meant a real difference in the trenches, soldiers reported, and, after the war ended, an appetite arose for dress shoes and boots made out of heavy-duty chrome-tanned leather. Demand for W&JM's Scotch Grain leathers began to grow in the U.K. and Europe. Sensing that this trend would catch on in the U.S., as our soldiers came marching home, my grandfather, Hermann Loewenstein, initiated a working relationship with W&JM and started to import their leathers. Sales really took off in 1924, and when Dad entered HL a year later, he was put in charge of sales of Scotch Grain in the U.S. This responsibility included visiting the tannery in Scotland on a regular basis and traveling annually with his counterpart, Douglas "Dougal" Martin, to visit our U.S. customers. Dad and Douglas often brought their wives along when they made these trips across the Atlantic, depositing them at each other's homes as the men tended to business, at the tannery and on the road.

Over time, a strong, lasting friendship developed, between the two men and their wives. I remember with fondness the visits Douglas and his wife made to our home in Great Neck. I can picture Anne – we called her Auntie Anne – singing and dancing with us kids and Douglas – Uncle Dougal to us – regaling us with some of his stories. There was something special about this friendship that linked the couples, the wives and the two men together. As I was growing up, it was fun and comforting to see how they so thoroughly enjoyed, trusted and loved each other.

This being the case, it's of little wonder that when Dad hatched his plan for me and Dave, he picked W. & J. Martin's tannery in Glasgow as the place for us to get our feet wet and our hands dirty. The Martins, after all were already like family to me, and Dad was sure we would be watched over and cared for. Douglas would see to it that Dave and I were well supervised and instructed at work. Anne would see to our needs during our visit to Troon, a small town 35 miles southeast of Glasgow. Both would offer advice and make sure we were safe, well prepared and provisioned for the rest of our cycling trip.

By the time our trip began, in late May of 1952, I had turned 17. I was ready, even anxious to learn something about tanning and eager to learn a bit about the world as well. The two-month journey Dad laid out was ingenious and appealing. Knowing of the close friendship I'd formed with Dave, he decided to check him out thoroughly to see if he might be a suitable traveling companion and workmate on this junket. To get a sense of his work ethic, Dad offered Dave a job during Christmas vacation in 1951. This kind of vetting was not unusual. Dad routinely offered jobs to pals of mine and friends of my sister Lenie. It was a great way to make my work stints at Loewenstein more fun and give Dad a good look-see at kids who might someday come to work for him.

Dave passed muster as expected, so Dad moved on to the next step of his plan, laying out our trip, contacting the people abroad who would be involved and coming up with a cost estimate. Dad was an expert at doing this, mapping out in great detail where we would go, what we would do and who we would see. This phase of his planning completed, he started contacting the people we would be seeing during our trip, individuals he felt he could rely on to succor us, guide us, keep us out of trouble and come to our aid if we got into a jam. The Martins, both Douglas and Anne, were his lynchpins. But there were others as well that he enlisted, and for good reasons, watchful eyes, open arms and one person who played an unexpected role, agent provocateur. With agreements to serve secured from all those he contacted and no logistical problems detected, Dad pulled the trigger. With Dave's dad on board, the trip was a go. We were ready for launch.

Our trip, in a way, was a rite of passage, certainly one of the most formative and memorable excursions I've had in my lifetime.

The next step was preparation, Both Dave and I were fit. Dave was a runner, a star on the track team at Great Neck High School. I was a football player, competing for a first-string position as left tackle on the Lawrenceville's state championship football team. We were also curious, an important attribute for anyone who wants to get the most out of their travels. And we were resourceful and not shy to ask for help. If we couldn't fix something that broke, we would find someone who could.

What we lacked was equipment, from soup to nuts. The first quite obvious thing was bikes. Up to now, Dave, I and the majority of our friends rode around our neighborhood on fat-wheeled Schwinns. Those bikes worked fine in this kind of setting but were clearly not what we needed to be riding on the kind of trip Dad envisioned for us. We needed a bike that would make hill climbing easier. We needed one that would go faster. We needed a Raleigh three-speed English racer. And that's what our dads bought us. It's been years since they made these investments in our futures, but I can still see that spiffy maroon colored Raleigh in my mind's eye. It was fitted to my height, so it was easy to pedal. The shifter worked smoothly and the brakes performed perfectly. I remember my pride and the joy when I first took it out for a spin. And Dad's confidence in me meant a lot.

Other things were also needed. Panniers and large backpacks were purchased to carry our gear. Clothing, utensils, toiletries and the other necessities we would need were identified and procured. By the time we left home, we were well prepared. Our eight-week trip to the U.K. could not be called an expedition, but for us it was an odyssey and we were ready to set sail.

Our trip began in New York City at Penn Station. The plan was for Dave and me to take a train to Baltimore where the Anchor Line freighter we would be boarding was taking on cargo. I rode in to the city with Mom and Dad. Dave's parents took him in. We met, had lunch at the station and then said goodbye to our parents. Details of this farewell are blurry, but I can feel the hug Mom gave me, hear the pep talk I got from Dad and see their vigorous waves as our train left the station. And then we were off, out of the nest, on our own.

As the train rumbled out of its first stop in Newark, a couple of younger kids who had boarded the train with us in New York got up the courage to ask us a few questions. They had spotted our English racers and were, I guess, envious. They wanted to know all about those sleek machines. We told them and, after a few moments, they asked us where we were going. We told them Scotland and gave them a short synopsis of what we would be doing and a thumbnail sketch of the route we were planning to take, cycling through the Highlands of Scotland and south, through England, to Southampton. Their eyes were wide with excitement. "Wow," they said in awe. Their mother sitting in the row behind them chimed in and asked, "How old are you?" "17 and 18," we replied. "That's quite young for a trip like the one you told my boys you are taking? Have your parents really thought this one through?" she continued, expressing growing concern. "I think they have." I told her. "My dad has lots of friends in Scotland and England. We know who to call if we have difficulties." "Yes, but what about here, in the U.S., on the Baltimore waterfront?" her husband interjected. "You told my sons you're leaving from there by freighter. Right? Well, if your ship sails tomorrow, you'll be on the waterfront tonight. That's not a place I'd want my sons to be and, for sure, not at night. The two of you look like you can take care of yourselves, but, be careful! The men who work as stevedores on the waterfront are a pretty rough crowd," he concluded, with gravity. "We'll be careful," we replied, without really having the knowledge or fear of what might be facing us on the Baltimore waterfront that evening.

The other incident occurred as our train left Princeton Junction. A fleeting memory of me detraining there during my first year at Lawrenceville shot into my head from nowhere. My experience in its Lower School as a member of Thomas House had not been an easy one – lots of bullying, not uncommon in prep school. It was something I would get over but still needed to work on as I returned to school in January after Christmas break. When I'd started at Lawrenceville in September of 1950, Mom and Dad had driven me down. This time they put me on the LIRR in Great Neck. I was on my own, detraining at Penn Station and getting aboard a Pennsylvania Railroad train headed for Washington. D.C. Dad had prebooked my ticket with the agency he used for his business travel. I had it in my hands along with a PRR timetable for this route. I knew how many stops the train would make before Princeton Junction. I knew when it would arrive there, but I was still nervous. Would I fall asleep and miss my stop? How long did the train stop at this minor waypoint? Would there be enough time for me to get my luggage from the rack and hop off? I made it all right that time, a notch in my belt. This time the challenges we would face, in the U.S. and abroad, would be far more complicated. But you know something, I told myself, you *are* ready to do this.

After clearing the railroad station in Baltimore, we hopped on our bikes and cycled down to the pier. The ship was set to sail the following day and was being loaded with its cargo when we arrived that afternoon. Watching the process was quite interesting. These days, cargo is shipped in a container. In 1952, that technology was still being perfected. Some container ships were being built. But our freighter was not one of them and it took quite a while to load it with cargo. It would not be until 1956 that a container ship landed at any U.S. port and many years more, before one sailed into a dredged and deepened Baltimore harbor. When we arrived dockside, huge nets, loaded with wooden crates, were being put into position for cranes to pick them up, swing their loads 90 degrees from the dock to ship deck, and once properly positioned, lower their contents into the huge holds on the ship. The jobs being worked by the longshoremen and the ship's crew were dangerous, in some cases backbreaking, requiring skilled operators, willing to take the risks involved. The men that worked were tough. They needed to be.

When we arrived on the pier in the late afternoon, we were welcomed by the crew member supervising the loading operations. He told us we could not stay aboard until loading was finished but asked if we wanted to leave our gear, including our bikes, in our cabin for safekeeping. That seemed to be a good idea and we took him up on it. He also gave us a tip about where to eat, a restaurant within walking distance and told us about a strip joint not much further away. He suggested we grab a bite at that restaurant, hang out at the strip joint until about 8 P.M. and then return to the ship. That sounded like good advice. We took it and were on our way.

The food at the restaurant was not special, but it was satisfying. Our visit to the strip joint was as well. Playboy, with its graphic centerfolds, would launch the following year. That degree of nudity would be new, titillating. But there had been plenty of girlie magazines circulating in my dorm at Lawrenceville. The naked female body was not a mystery. I'd seen plenty of curvaceous cuties in the dogeared magazines that wound up on the coffee table in our room. And I liked what I saw. No question. But seeing girls strip, up close, that was a new experience for me. The room was smoky. Slow, suggestive music was playing as the girls were swaying. A long mirror with a gilded frame, hung on the back wall and a wide, varnished, wooden bar was positioned just in front of it. The scene looked like something straight out of a western. On the bar, which ran from one wall to the other, were girls, buxom young ladies in various stages of undress. I sensed the mood in that room as we bellied up to the bar. It was almost feral. There were raucous cries of "take it off, take it off." There were hands reaching up to stuff money into the cleavage of the girls who were still wearing bras. There were men with glassy eyes, hungry, expectant, staring at the spectacle. The image was visceral, provocative, hard to forget. We spent an hour there and left somewhat the wiser, reentering the world we had come from, the waterfront. It was scary in a number of ways, as audiences watching Marlon Brando in *On the Waterfront* would attest when that movie was released two years later. But it was quiet that night, not threatening and less unsettling than the world from which we had just departed. When we returned to our ship, loading was still underway at another vessel nearby. The cranes were wheeling around and there was shouting. A poker game was underway on the pier as we boarded the HMS Whatchamacallit. We stopped briefly to watch it as we headed to our cabin. There was action but we were tired. Our stomachs were full, we'd downed enough beer and seen enough bare flesh for one night. We were sated, safe and ready for bed.

The Boat Ride Over

The next day, as our ship prepared to sail, we met the captain and our fellow passengers. There were four other souls, an English couple in their late thirties, early forties, and their two sons, ages around 10 and 12. They were as new to ocean travel as we were. None of us had ever made an Atlantic crossing, much less on a freighter. As we sailed out of Baltimore harbor, none of us had any idea of what to expect. Meals, we learned quickly, were served to the six of us in a small wardroom. The food was tasty and ample but definitely not fine dining. Other than meals, nothing was offered to passengers. Entertainment was a do-it-yourself enterprise. This was not a cruise ship or an ocean liner. It lacked the amenities and entertainment those vessels provide their passengers. There were no movies, lectures or shows, no bar or pool. We were left to entertain ourselves. And so we made our own fun. We played board, card and word games. Sometimes just Dave and I were involved; other times members of the English family joined in. A popular diversion was hide and seek. It sounds kind of weird, guys our age, playing hide and seek. But with nothing better to do, watching those two young kids scurry around, finding places to hide, got to be fun. When their parents took part, hide and seek became even more interesting. Watching the couple play, laugh and celebrate with their kids was heartwarming. Besides exercise, it also gave us all a chance to thoroughly explore the ship. Occasionally we went a step too far, hiding or seeking in restricted areas. There were some reprimands when we did, but by and large the captain and his crew were understanding and forgiving of our overzealous pioneering.

Another feature of our voyage. one that mesmerized me, was the ocean. It was an omnipresent reality and, for me at least, an undeniable attraction. I had done a lot of sailing before we left Baltimore on this passage, but I was unprepared for what I saw the first time I went to the bow and sat down. That expanse of water before me stretched to the horizon. There would be no land in sight for seven days. The sea was a deeper blue than what I'd ever seen in Manhasset Bay or on Long Island Sound. At times it was a milky teal, others when it turned to gray as clouds scudded over or hid the sun. The ever-changing architecture of the sea was like the wave patterns I'd experienced at home but on a much larger scale. Sometimes there was dead calm, sometimes I could see the catspaws Dad always looked for when he was racing. There were days when all you could see were whitecaps with winds so strong that even Dad would have to reef his sails or strip them and head for port.

We never experienced a day of really heavy weather. This allowed me to spend countless, happy hours in the bow of our freighter. Lying on my stomach, head craned upward as I focused on the horizon, looking for the appearance of a ship or maybe a first sighting of a land mass. Head down, feeling and hearing the ship pound its way through the waves, I sensed I was part of it, not just on it, as I watched the wide, white, foamy wake it was creating. On occasion, I saw a school of dolphins frolicking in that froth. At others, as we neared a land mass, I would spy sea birds.

I'd never been seasick, even when sailing in foul weather, but the ship's slow, rhythmic movement, up and down, side to side was different. It got to me at first and made me queasy. Fortunately, that didn't last. I soon found my sea legs and when I did, the ship's pitch and roll comforted rather than bothered me. Other senses awakened in me; the salt air smelled good; the deep, sonorous hoot of the ship's horn was almost musical. I thrive when engaged in interesting conversations and activities. But here, lying all alone, in the bow of that ship, I needed no one to talk to, nothing more than what my eyes, ears and nose were experiencing and telling me. I felt at peace with the world.

We arrived in Liverpool on a gray, rainy day, a suitable introduction to the moist, "soft" weather we would encounter while cycling in Great Britain. We hugged the members of the English family as we parted company. We would never see or hear from them again but they had been good company during our Atlantic crossing. We disembarked and were off to the railroad station on our bikes. The next leg of our itinerary was train travel from Liverpool to Glasgow, departing from the Lime Street station, five miles from the port. With tickets prebought, some English money in our pockets and a small city map in hand, we were ready to roll. We were not ready, however, for the rubble we saw en route to the train station. It was a sobering experience. Liverpool had been severely bombed by the Luftwaffe during World War II. Rebuilding of the areas that had been badly damaged, was still in progress. We had watched wartime newsreels when we went to the movies. We had seen pictures and read stories about the horrors of war. But that war took place "over there" and ended seven years ago. Seeing the rebuilding what remained to be done I realized just how lucky we were in the United States of America.

Trains from Liverpool to Glasgow run frequently these days. They take from just under four hours to over seven hours depending on how many stops they make. Given the damage to British rail during the war and the improvement in the engines and cars of today, I'd guess it took us over eight hours to get to Glasgow. A warm welcome awaited us as we got off the train. Bill Martin, five years our senior, a relative of the Martin brothers who owned the W. & J. Martin tannery, had been dispatched to meet us and to act as our trainer during our two-week stint at the tannery. He was a trainee himself, still learning the ropes, but it was instantly clear he knew more than enough to put us through our paces. He was looking forward to the task he had been given, teaching two young Yanks how to tan leather. His sense of humor was coupled with an appreciation for the rigor of work in a tannery. This demeanor earned him good rapport with the crusty Scotsmen with whom we would be working and proved invaluable during our training. His advice to us was spot on: "Work hard and safely, keep your eyes and ears open, ask questions but don't whine. You'll be welcomed and respected if you do." We did just that and became one of the crew, precisely as he had predicted. He became a role model during our training and a lifelong friend, from that day forward.

Tannery Trainees – Two Weeks in the Wet End at W&JM

Workers in leather tanneries, aka leather mills, are quite well paid. Given the conditions in which they work, these "mill rats", as they are often referred to, deserve these higher-than-average pay checks. This is true, especially in the "wet end" where raw hides are turned into a non-perishable commodity. And that's where we spent our two weeks training, on the night shift, working in the wet end.

At W&JM, the steer and ox hides it processes were delivered to its hide house, folded, tied into bundles averaging 70+ lbs. in weight and piled, two to three rows high, on wooden pallets. When called for, these, bundles would be opened, trimmed and cut along their backbones into sides and moved into the "beamhouse" for processing. Dave and I watched as the heads and shanks of these hides were cut off and the hide was sided. As they travel through the tannery these sides will be fleshed, split and shaved. All are machine operations in which these peripheral appendages might get caught in the jaws of the machine, damaging the side and potentially causing severe injury to its operator. Good judgment as to what to trim off is required. After seeing how it was done, Dave and I were given a trimming knife and told to have a go. Our teacher, the lead trimmer, was impressed. We had passed our first test and the word got around.

The first step in the leather making process is soaking, a 15-20 hour immersion in a paddle vat. Its large wooden paddles rotate, slowly, much like the paddlewheels on old river boats, churning the sides, softening and washing them clean of foreign matter, including the salt used to cure them. Our job was simple but required upper body strength; from the stacks of 50 or so sides, piled, hair up on pallets, we picked up them up, one at a time, and threw them into the paddle vat. And then, after they had been soaked and cleaned, we pulled them out of the vat, one by one, and stacked them, hair side up, on a pallet that would be taken over to the fleshing machine. We worked in rubber boots, wore long rubber aprons and gloves. Our eyes were protected with plastic safety goggles. There was nothing dangerous about what we were doing but, oh my, our muscles sure ached after an eight-hour shift loading and pulling sides out of those vats. It was an introduction to tanning I'll never forget!

Once "soaked back," the flesh, fat and muscle remaining on the back side of these sides is scraped off by the bladed roller in fleshing machine. We delivered the sides to the fleshing machine but were not asked to try our hand at operating this machine. Instead, we happily embraced the role of student, watching a master ply his craft. I winced slightly, imagining myself doing this job as the operator deftly swung a side into the jaws of the machine, pushed a button that closed its jaws, started the bladed roller rotating, gripped both edges of the side, and guided it as it was being fed out of the machine.

The next step was dehairing and liming. This is done in a paddle vat filled with an aqueous solution containing hydrated lime and sodium sulfide. These chemicals dissolve the hair on these sides and swell them up in preparation for the next steps, scudding, bating and pickling. Scudding was done by hand in 1952 when we were in training at W&JM. The purpose of this process is to remove any dissolved hair particles remaining in the hair follicles of the side. This was done by draping the side, grain up, over a curved "beam." Then, using a dull bladed curved knife that was fitted to the curvature of the beam and placing it at the top of the beam, pressure is applied on the grain as the knife is pushed to the bottom of the beam. Dave and I tried our hand at this operation. It was quite exciting watching the colored juice of dissolved hair spurt out of hair follicles and run down the side as we ran the knife to the end of the beam. It was another accomplishment, showing our willingness to do some dirty work, gaining us even more respect from our Scottish mates. I felt rather proud of myself and, at the same time, somewhat sorry for the men who did this backbreaking job on a steady basis.

The bating process follows. It starts with deliming which lowers the sides' pH, reduces swelling and prepares them for the bating enzymes. These are introduced to digest undesirable constituents in the grain side (epidermis) of the hide which, if not removed, will harden and make its surface "tinny" (brittle). These enzymes are fed through the hollow axle of a large, wooden drum that rotates on its axle, keeping the sides in it in constant motion. Our job here was to load and unload these drums. Nothing too strenuous since by now the sides were lighter and easier to handle, a definite plus.

Pickling followed, in which the sides' pH starts turning acidic, preparing them for chrome tanning, splitting, shaving, coloring and fat liquoring, the last of four steps performed in a tannery's wet end. And that's about as far as we got in 1952, to the tail end of the "wet end". The dry area, where toggling, pasting, and vacuum drying are used to dry and stretch sides to their maximum area after they have been colored and fat liquored. These were all day shift jobs so we did not do any of them. But we came in one day and walked through these areas observing how sides were finished, embossed, sorted and packed. Once again, we were only observers. Actually doing these jobs came later when I became a trainee in our tannery in Gloversville in 1964.

Thinking back to our days at W&JM, one incident in particular makes me smile. It happened on a night we were loading and unloading color drums. The crew was small and Bill decided to smuggle in his HMV gramophone so we could listen to some records while we worked. We had two jobs to do that night. The first was loading chrome tanned sides into the large wooden drums in which they would be colored and fat liquored. "Wet blue" hides have a distinct, acrid smell which permeates your clothing and irritates your nose. Their odor is not pleasant and it's hard to get rid of, but that night we were in a good mood and hardly noticed it. Once sides are colored and fat-liquored, the pungent smell is totally gone, replaced by a much more pleasant odor. In this process, dyes, natural and synthetic, turn the "wet blue" sides into whatever color and degree of softness a customer desires. In later years when I was working at our tannery in Gloversville, we dyed our leathers to all colors of the rainbow. Here at W&JM, the color palette was much diminished.

With Bill's music in the background, time went by swiftly and at 6 A.M. when our shift was done, we left the tannery at 42 Baltic St. and headed to the tram stop at Bridgeton Cross. It was only a few minutes' walk away and, with the sun already risen, our spirits remained high. On arriving at the stop, we decided we needed more music, so we sat down on the pavement, put another record onto Bill's gramophone and turned it on. The record of choice this time was Les Paul and Mary Ford's "How High the Moon," a favorite of Dave's. We sang along, providing unexpected amusement for the other passengers waiting for the tram. The electrified green and yellow No. 3 tram we would be taking started its route at Glasgow University on the other side of the city, crossed the River Clyde, then started up the hill towards Bridgeton Cross and terminated at Bellahouston Park, site of the 1938 International Trade Fair. We didn't go to the end of the line that night. We jumped off, to applause, at a stop halfway up the hill, in Pollokshields, and from there walked a few blocks to the Maxwell Hotel, our home during those two weeks. This massive red sandstone structure, one of many similar buildings nearby, was a good example of the style of architecture that dominated much of Glasgow at the time. The common rooms were spacious and well appointed. The bedrooms were high-ceilinged and commodious. The only thing lacking was an elevator, a missing link we endured unconsciously, as we climbed the two flights of stairs that led to our room and plopped, happily, into bed.

Bike Ride Through the Highlands

Our two-week apprenticeship in the tannery successfully completed, we said goodbye to Bill, hopped onto our three-speed bicycles and headed north into the Scottish Highlands. It was to be a six-day trip, punctuated with stops each night at youth hostels. Working with Douglas Martin and Friedel Simon, another business friend who lived south of London, Dad began to scope out a route for us that the three men felt would be interesting, doable and safe. Douglas and Friedel had firsthand knowledge of youth hosteling in the U.K. This movement, founded in 1931, had been affected by the war but the three men mapping out our travels deemed it operational and essential to their plans for us. Dormitories were what these hostels offered, and while the quality of the accommodations varied, their research gave them comfort that any of the ones they had vetted along the route they were plotting for us would be safe. What's more, they were not expensive, charging only a shilling for a one-night stay.

With Dad convinced that staying in hostels was a pragmatic decision, the next step was mapping an actual route. This phase of their planning most certainly involved choosing places with scenic things to see along the way. Equally important, if not more important, was the choice of end-of-the-day destinations, each of which had to boast a hostel and be a manageable distance from the previous destination. And how far should that be? After deciding that two strapping guys like Dave and I would have no problem cycling six to eight hours a day, they concluded that if we averaged around 15–20 mph, we should be able to do 100–125 miles in a day. So that was set as a daily maximum. With that assumption agreed upon, our route through the Highlands was drawn up, agreed upon and fixed.

In later years, Dad's dictation of paths I should follow caused me resentment, resulting in passive-aggressive behavior that sapped my energy as well as my resolve. Had this been the case in 1952, the route he planned for us might not have been followed. Dad's calculus of up to 125 miles per day based on our fitness and focus might also have proved unrealistic. But these were early days. Dad's wishes had not as yet come across as demands. I was ready to roll, in very good shape and definitely more eager to rack up miles on my bike than to stop and linger at tourist attractions.

Since Dave and I did not keep logs and only one of the photos I took still exists, a picture of Dave sitting near his bike by the side of a road in front of a pasture. Where that was I have no idea and, to be honest. the exact route we took is a matter of conjecture. But I feel confident, that the one I'll be describing is a credible replica of our travels. Here's what I did that gives me that confidence. The first was to buy National Geographic maps of Scotland and England. The ones I bought were large topographical maps, big enough to see all major roads, lochs, mountains, cities, towns and even some of the small villages. The maps were covered with a plastic laminate, a real plus, making it possible for me to fold them into quadrants I could fit onto my desk top for closer examination. As I examined these maps, I looked for names that seemed familiar, of lochs and lakes, large and small I might have ridden by, of cities, towns and villages I could have stayed in overnight or cycled through, and of mountains I might have seen in the distance. It took a while to get properly oriented. Gradually, as other place names got added to my list of familiars, I was ready to link these waypoints together by roadways. And, lo and behold, a route map of our bike trip through the Highlands and down the spine of England started to develop.

The next step was trying to identify destinations. In which of the myriad of waypoints on this hypothetical route, might we have spent a night? One thing stuck out as I tried to come up with some logical answers – an aha moment. We stayed only in youth hostels, didn't we? Bingo! I had something with which to vet a possible destination. There had to be a hostel in this city, town or village. And if there was none? Well, we didn't stay there.

With Google at my side, readying me for the task of identifying the presence of hostels, I could now validate a destination. This was a nice leap forward, but before I could begin to construct a definitive route map, I needed to factor in one more constraint, the distances between destinations. I need to make sure that the distance between point A and point B, point B and point C, point C and point D, etc., could be no greater than the amount of ground Dave and I could cover in a day. And just how far might that be? If we were adhering to Dad's calculus, 125 miles would be the most we would travel in the course of a day. That sounded logical to me, but before I set my dividers to measure 125 miles on my maps, I decided to call a couple of bike shops to validate Dad's assumptions. Both shops felt that 125 miles per day was a bit high, but doable. A Google search confirmed this. It indicated that a good average was somewhere around 65 miles per day but noted that an experienced rider in good condition could cover 120 miles in a day. Dave and I were fit. We had new English racers. They match the capabilities of today's racing bikes, like the 2021 sleek 10-speed Iannarelli Dogma FL for example, but they were speedy and spiffy. And we were men on a mission! It may be a stretch, but I think we could have handled the distances between waypoints I've projected and stayed overnight where I've reckoned we did. Based on this hypothesis I've reconstructed our route and described our days as we biked through the Highlands, the Lake District and down the spine of England.

With these constraints in mind, I started scouring the maps I'd purchased. Putting my forefinger on Glasgow, I started moving it, first north through the Highlands, up to where I thought we went. From there I looked west, east, then back South again to Troon, which I knew was one of the last stops on our tour of Scotland, looking for cities, towns and villages that might have been on the route we biked in 1952. As I read the names on the map, I asked myself questions. Was I in Inverness on this trip? Yes was the answer to that; I'd been there in 1952 and many times thereafter. But no, I realized, was the correct answer when it came to Edinburgh and Perth. I'd been to both, but not on this trip. And what about towns with names like Dunblane, Pitlochry, Fort William? Yep, it sure seemed they were on this trip. And villages with unforgettable, unpronounceable names like Drumnadrochit, Dalwhinnie, Kingussie, Crianlarich? Did we pass through them in 1952? The fog started to lift and bells rang.

Day 1: Pollokshields via Pitlochry via Dunblane, Creiff and Dunkeld

87 MILES

On the first day of our bike trip, day 30 of our odyssey, we cycled from the Pollokshields section of Glasgow to Pitlochry, a journey of 85 miles on today's roads. This leg took us through the heart of Glasgow, the second largest city in the United Kingdom, home to greater than a million souls. There were no skyscrapers and the buildings we saw as we rode out of the city were mostly drab, three-and four-story stone structures. A heavily industrialized city, a deep-water port and a major shipbuilding center, Glasgow had suffered significant damage at the hands of the Luftwaffe. As was the case in Manchester, rebuilding was still underway in 1952, but it was mostly in the Port Glasgow area, west of the route we chose to take to Pitlochry.

Leaving Glasgow behind, we headed towards Stirling and Dunblane, then on to Crieff and Gilmerton. Here we entered Glen Almond and crossed paths, for the first of many times, with a flock of sheep, 50 or more of them, slowly meandering across the road. We'd been prepared for this. Scotland has more sheep than people. But the blue daubs of paint on their pelts, that was unexpected. Turns out, as the shepherd guiding this flock told us, farmers here in Scotland paint their animals instead of branding them. We thanked him for his explanation, stopped for several minutes as he guided his flock across the narrow road we were traveling and then pedaled on to Pitlochry

Our first day out had been a long one. We were tired when we arrived at our hostel but not ready for bed. A pint of beer and some fish and chips sounded good, so after checking in and placing our paniers on beds in our dormitory, we headed off to a nearby pub. Pitlochry, it turned out, was a gem of a town and its people, we found out quickly, were most welcoming. It had not yet become the tourist destination it is today, but ideas for ways to entertain visitors were already afoot. Plays were staged in in a tent each summer and plans for a larger, permanent theater complex and annual festival were being discussed. Today these ideas are a reality, and the local hotel and the B&Bs are full.

Day 2: Pitlochry–Inverness via Dahlwhinnie and Kingussie

88 MILES

The following morning, we set out early for Inverness, some 90 miles away. Taking the route I believe we took, Dahlwhinnie, Kingussie and Aviemore, names unique enough to be buried somewhere in my brain, started to bubble up. Assuming these bubbles were not misleading, they would have been villages we passed through as we made our way up the valley between two mountain ranges, the Monadhliath and Cairngorms. Traveling this way, at this time of year, I can imagine we would have seen some yellow gorse, purple thistle and other wildflowers on the hillsides. No doubt we would have also encountered flocks of sheep whose migrations, from one side of road to the other, gave us time to catch our breath and take sips of water from our canteens. Given the terrain we traveled through, my guess is that we would have had a long day and probably arrived in Inverness after 7 P.M. The skies would still be light since in Scotland, that far north, the sun sets well after 9 P.M. in the summer. Whether it was 9 P.M., earlier or later, our riding always made us hungry and thirsty. And so, without a doubt in my mind, I am sure we went off to a pub before we went to bed, had a pint of bitters and maybe a plate of shepherd's pie to tide us over till we arose in the morning for the next day's ride.

Day 3: Inverness–Gairloch via Garve, Inchabe and Dundonnell

98 MILES

Inverness, our departure point on day three, is an old city, settled before the sixth century A.D. Today it is the cultural capital of the Highlands and a mecca for tourists interested in history, architecture and natural beauty. To Dave and me, in 1952, it was little more than a way point, one, as it turned out, we visited twice. And we didn't have time to visit historical sites like Culloden or set foot in landmarks like the Free North Church, the Inverness Town House or the Wordlaw Mausoleum. Our time was limited and we had to move on. The leg we projected doing that day was one of the longest in our entire bike trip. We couldn't judge the distance as well as I can today using Google Maps, but we could see from the map we were working with that we had a long way to go. We didn't mind. We were pumped. The weather looked drizzly as we peeked out the window of our hostel, so we pulled our ponchos out of our paniers and off we went.

If I was planning to go to Gairloch by car today I would opt to cross the Beauly Firth on the Kessock Bridge. It's a magnificent piece of engineering and affords beautiful views as you cross it. Chloe and I would do so, many times when we visited Bill and Brenda Martin at their home on the Black Isle. That route would also have trimmed miles off the distance we needed to cycle. But that bridge, a fixture now, was yet to be built. We must have gone another way. The route I can imagine we traveled headed due West out of Inverness, skirting the Beauly Firth and connected with what is now the A832 just south of Beauly. Following this road to just north of Garve, it looks like we would probably have veered off to the right, onto the A835 and then, south of Braemore, taken the left fork at the eastern end of Little Loch Broom, towards Dundonnell. Continuing northwest on the southern bank of this loch, we would have started bending west, near its western end and then due south on this road, to the eastern end of Gruinard Bay. Keeping the bay on our right we must have cycled on to Laide and from there headed south along the eastern shore of Loch Ewe towards Londubh. Are you still with me? Not much further to go. From here there's a wee leg, going south, southeast to Poolewee, and finally, a slightly longer stretch southwest to the northeast shore of Gairloch. Hold on, we're almost there, just one more turn, to the left, and a short run southeast along Gairloch's eastern shore to Charlestown.

Are you exhausted? Actually, we were not. We were lucky, very lucky that day; we got a comfortable car ride, most of the way. I see us riding through Inchbae and cycling along the southern shore of Loch Glascarnoch. It was raining, not just drizzling, when a solicitous older couple passed us and then came to a stop on what was then a very narrow two-lane road with occasional laybys. They were driving a smallish four-door sedan, towing a camping trailer, headed to Gairloch on vacation. When they offered to give us a lift you can imagine how long it took us to accept it. Milliseconds! We stowed our bikes in their van, hopped into their car and off we went, riding with them all the way to Charlestown. Getting that lift was a godsend and they were angels! We rode, dry and warm, past beautiful scenery and water. We also thoroughly enjoyed their company, an added plus. In today's world, hitchhiking is not as common as it was back then. Scots are warm, welcoming people but I have my doubts that an older couple like the ones who gave us this ride would stop to pick up a couple of bedraggled bikers like us. As it was, they seemed to have a grand old time with the two young Yanks to whom they had offered a lift. And Dave and I, we couldn't have been happier to travel with them and hear their stories.

Day 4: Gairloch-Inverness
via Talladale, Kinlochewe, Achnasheen and Garve

70 MILES

Day 4 of our trip through the Highlands took us from Gairloch through Talladale, Kinlochewe, Achnasheen and Garve, back to Inverness. We were lucky. The weather had turned better. There was sunshine as we rode along the shore of Loch Maree. I remembered it as one of the most beautiful bodies of water in the western Highlands and, when I got one of the many postcards Bill sent me to illustrate our bike trip, I knew that others who've seen it, must feel the same way. I was captivated and must confess it was my memory of riding by that loch that anchored my yet unformed vision of where Dave and I had gone on the Scottish portion of our bike trip. The roadway we were on started climbing as we approached Incheril at the eastern end of the loch, a memory confirmed by National Geographic map I was using as a guide as I was writing this portion of my book. One detail, however, was dissonant, a cable car that was depicted near the town of Kinglochewe. My sense is that it wasn't there when we rode by in 1952. I can imagine the temptation we might have had, to get off our bikes and take a ride to the top of it. If time had not been of the essence, I'm sure that we'd have been tempted. And done it. But we didn't and as describe our day and what we'd seen, I wish we had.

Enough dreaming; let's get back in the saddle and finish the story of what happened that day. At Incheril we turned left and headed due east to Achnasheen. Here we took another left, a slight one, following the Bran River, to Achana, Loch Luichart and on to Corriemoille. And at that juncture with the A835, just above Garve, we got on this road and retraced, in reverse, the steps to Inverness we had taken the day before. It had been a long day with quite a bit of climbing. We were tired, I'm sure, ate a quick dinner and climbed into bed, resting up for day 5 of our journey.

Day 5: Inverness, Fort William
via Drumnadrochit, Fort Augustus and Invergarry
67 MILES

We left Inverness early that morning. The weather was still fine. We noticed on our map that there were two castles on the route we planned, Urquhart Castle, one third of the way down the western shore of Loch Ness, through Fort Augustus and on to Inverlochy Castle where the River Lochy flows into Loch Eil. We knew that we did not have time to take tours, but we didn't want to whiz by either. We were also told to keep an eye out for Nessie, the mythical monster who is said to live in this loch. Since we were riding so close to its western shore, we couldn't avoid taking an occasional peek over our left shoulder to see if he was sporting about. No such luck. But we did stop to see the castles and they were impressive. It was relatively easy ride that day, only 67 miles with, a number of stops along the way, mostly photo ops of these castles taken from afar. Pulling into Fort William too late to visit any of its tourist attractions, we checked into our hostel and went out to eat at an outdoor café that provided us with an unobstructed view of Ben Nevis, Scotland's highest mountain. As we finished our dinner and took last sips from our pints of porter, we looked to the east to see it slowly change color as the last rays of sunshine faded away. What a way to end a day!

Day 6: Fort William–Tarbet
via Glencoe, Tyndrum and Crianlarich

68 MILES

The distance we traveled on Day 6, from Fort William to Tarbet on the shores of Loch Lomond was another short run. It was also one of the most challenging we faced in the Highlands, peppered with plenty of hill climbing. It started out easy as we rode down the eastern shore of Loch Linnhe to Onich. Here the road looped around a bay and crossed a bridge in North Ballachulish at the western end of Loch Leven. From there we started pedaling into the historic valley of Glencoe, the legendary home of Fingal, one of the greatest Celtic heroes, a leader of the Fein, warriors of Gaelic mythology. We knew nothing of this story as we made our way through a breathtaking passage, literally and physically, between mini mountains, called Munros. We were breathing hard as we climbed up the pass, reached the top, and took in the views on the other side As I traced this route on my map, I could imagine what we must have been seeing, but to help me better experience this moment, I did a Google search prior to writing these lines. Revealed on my computer screen were pictures, gorgeous ones of the road we traveled, a synopsis of the Fingal legend and the fact that Mendelssohn had written a piece of music, the "Hebrides Overture," aka "Fingal's Cave," putting that story to music. Knowing that, I dialed in a YouTube video to listen to this haunting overture as I was typing these lines. The experience was extraordinary What a treat to an aspiring writer, what a spur to a happy memory, all bestowed to me by modern technology.

As we pedaled forward to the end of our day's journey, here's a tale within a tale. When I struggled, years later, to break away from the plans my father laid for me, I was often faced with an inner struggle. Should I go with my gut and follow a path of my own choosing or should I take the easy way out and not argue with my dad about the path he wanted me to take. While cycling on towards Tyndrum, Dave and I faced that sort of a decision. At Crianlarich, at the northern end of Loch Lomond, the road forked. The right fork, skirting its western shore, would take us to Tarbet, to a hostel where Dad and Douglas expected us to stay. The left fork, hugging the eastern shore, appeared to be another option. Our map showed a dotted line that ran from Crianlarich to Rowardennan, a village that lay at the foot of Ben Lomond. Were these the two roads, the low road and the high road, that Andrew Lang popularized in his poem about Loch Lomond? If so, according to Lang, the low road was faster. But which of the two roads was the low road and should we take it, even if it did not lead us to the hostel in Tarbet where we were supposed to be going?

At the hostel in Fort William, I'd seen a picture of the hostel in Rowardennan. Over dinner the night before, I had overheard some mountain climbers speak of their plans to go there. It sounded appealing. The route to the southern end of Loch Lomond on this side of the loch looked to be the shorter of the two roads. So why not take it, even if that meant we would be going against Dad's wishes and the plan he and Douglas Martin had so carefully figured out for us? This seemed like the perfect opportunity to spread our wings, a minor diversion that they needn't ever know about?

There was research to be done, wasn't there, before we made this decision? We were ready to take off, but before pulling the trigger, we decided to check with one of the locals. I'm glad we did. In no uncertain terms we were told that the road on the west bank was the low road, the only road we should be taking if we intended to cycle along the bonnie banks of Loch Lomond. I leaned on my friend Bill Martin to help me reconstruct our interchange. Here's what Bill imagines might have been said to us. "Where are you lads frae?" Our accents as we replied were not hard to spot and the local man's face lit up with a smile as he heard our replies. "Oh, from Yankee land! Have you been here long with these fancy bikes?" We told him about our travels through the Highlands and how we had come to Scotland by freight steamer. He was impressed. "You're fitter than you look. Where are ye headin? Oh, the hostel. Weel, lads," he said with a smile, "the East Highland Way is bonnie, but it's nae built for sannies (aka sneakers). Take the road on the West Bank. It's the low road, but it's bonnie too. Your legs and your sannies will thank you if you do. And hae nae worries, you'll see all you could want of Loch Lomond and Ben Lomond across the way." And so, following our new friend's advice, we took what was now officially designated as the low road and sped on, to Tarbet, where we had a good night's rest.

Day 7: Tarbet–Troon
via Dumbarton, Paisley and Kilmarnock
63 MILES

Our destination the next day, approximately 60 miles away, was Dunchattan, the home of Douglas and Anne Martin, in Troon, located on the Firth of Clyde. We'd covered over 500 miles by the time we got there on that sunny Saturday afternoon. It was time to kick back, cool down and rest our weary legs. And rest we did as we relaxed in Dunchattan's airy living room and gathered as family, in its spacious dining room for meals and stories. Our visit felt like a homecoming to me and perhaps it was. Fanciful though it may seem, I think there are connections between me, the Martin family and not improbably, their home. The first inkling of this possibility was the fact that my parents chose to name me Roderick, shortened to Roddy in my youth and Rod later on. Both branches of my family are German and there are no Rodericks, Roddys or Rods anywhere in my family tree. So why did they hang that name on me, an appellation that encouraged no end of teasing as I was growing up?

The other curious coincidence had to do with the timing of my birth. I was born on May 12th, 1935, about nine months after Mom and Dad visited the Martins in Troon. Could I have been conceived under their roof? As was often the case in the early days of their marriage, Mom frequently accompanied Dad as he visited his suppliers and customers. This trip to Europe and the U.K. was one of many he took before their marriage and after they were wed. They were diversions that both seemed to enjoy. In a way, however, this particular trip was special, an opportunity to introduce his new bride to old friends, Douglas and Anne. The Martins were, without question, special, lifelong friends of both Mom and Dad. Their home was special for me as well, in more ways than one.

This being the case, it's not surprising that our interlude at Dunchattan was an extraordinary affair for me, a homecoming if you will. It was an opportunity to strengthen and expand the already vibrant relationship that already existed between my parents, with Douglas and Anne, and a chance for me to meet and connect with their children. Gatherings that allowed us to get to know one another occurred frequently during our two days at Dunchattan. These occurred especially at mealtimes when Douglas and Anne regaled us with stories as we sat around their large dining room table. A touching tale, related by Douglas, was how Mom and Dad had sent them regular CARE packages for several years after World War II. Severe food rationing was instituted during that war and lasted for quite a while after peace returned. These shipments of foodstuffs, clothing and incidentals were apparently needed and greatly appreciated. I had met the Martins and knew about their close relationship with my parents, but neither Mom or Dad had never told me about these shipments. Given the Martins' wealth and connections, I had assumed that they wanted for nothing. I was quite surprised then, to learn how difficult times had been for them and what a difference these CARE packages made.

Another vignette, this one told by Anne, is one I'll never forget. It's too delicious! As she served Dave and me a delectable poached salmon, Anne told us about an experience she once had fishing for salmon. The picture she painted was graphic, easy to imagine and enjoy. Here she was fly fishing, knee deep in the River Dee, on a stretch not far from Balmoral Castle. As she was preparing to cast towards a pool where she had spotted a rise, she noticed something else. It was Queen Elizabeth, walking briskly down a road on the castle grounds, on the opposite side of the river. Ever the lady, Auntie Anne, aware that she was about-to-be waterlogged, curtsied to her queen as soon as she saw her. And then, as coolish water coursed into her waders, she smiled graciously. These gestures, well above and beyond any call of duty, she learned later, did not go unnoticed. In curtseying midriver, showing extraordinary fealty to her queen, both she and Queen Elizabeth had a wonderful story to tell.

Another fond memory is of Uncle Dougal, working with his dogs, golden and black Labrador Retrievers, Brora and Suzie. That they had been extraordinarily well-trained, not only for the field, but also at table, became crystal clear as we sat at lunch and watched Douglas work with them. One of the lessons he had taught them was the importance of delayed gratification, a lesson both of them showed, moments later, that they had learned. As the meal progressed and rolls were passed around, Douglas took an extra one and put it next to his plate. Suzie and Brora, seeing the proximity of this prize and expecting the reward that might eventually be bestowed, looked up at their master with expectant eyes. Douglas looked back at them and slowly dismembered his extra roll. That done, Douglas commanded them to sit as he put a fragment of roll between his thumb and forefinger. Then, as the two dogs raised themselves to a sit position, he said the magic words "on trust" and placed fragments of roll on their noses. You could see Suzie and Brora's noses quiver, but both held steady. After a minute or so, Douglas brought this bit of theater to a close. Hearing the words "pay for," Bora and Suzie flipped the roll fragments in the air, deftly caught and swallowed them and returned to their prone positions.

In later years, Chloe and I had the pleasure of joining Douglas and Anne on a pheasant shoot on one of the Scottish estates where this sport is provided. To someone who had watched duck hunters shooting from blinds floating offshore on Manhasset Bay, bird hunting, Scottish style, was a totally different experience. Being included in their company, at play in this beautifully orchestrated spectacle, shooting, sipping sherry and nibbling at delicious watercress and cucumber sandwiches, was a real treat. Of particular joy was watching Suzie and Brora, now acting as bird dogs, responding to their master's commands. We had dogs when I was growing up. They were beloved members of our family, well fed, cared for and trained, but never, ever, did we ask them to perform like Suzie and Brora. There were lessons to be learned, watching Douglas, Suzie and Brora work as a team. These transcended what I had seen at the Martins' table and in the field, making me think as I write this book, what I might have done differently, as a parent, a businessman and a dog owner.

Besides the impression Anne and Douglas made on us with their stories and tricks, there were myriad other things that made our visit to Dunchattan so memorable. Meeting the next generation of Martins, Anne and Douglas's three daughters, Anne, Agnes-Mary and Alison, added an extra layer to the bond between the Correll and Martin clans. Today only Alison, the youngest, is alive. Still a fond but distant friend, Alison married Jeremy Gibbs, son of Southern Rhodesia's penultimate governor, Sir Humphrey Gibbs. I reached out to Alison as I was writing this story in hopes she might remember our visit to Dunchattan. She didn't, a minor blow to my ego since I can swear she was there. But she does remember, quite vividly, coming to the U.S. three or four years later and visiting my parents' home in Plandome Manor. Her recall of my running over a skunk en route to an event at Yale does bring back memories, faint ones, compared to a much stronger one about her visit to our home in Johnstown many years later. It was Halloween at the time of her visit. Trick-or-treaters were beating a path to our door on South William Street as we finished our drinks in the living room. As the first one at the front door, a tiny tot dressed up as a ballerina, uttered those magic words, trick or treat, Alison smiled mischievously and shot right back. "Do a trick for us, will you dear. We'll be sure to give you a treat if you do" I can't remember exactly what happened next, but if memory serves, we were treated to a pirouette, followed by an extended hand into which we deposited a candy bar.

Besides people, there were places that made our visit to Dunchattan so memorable. One of my most vivid memories is of the gardens at Dunchattan. Anne Martin had an incredibly inventive mind and a green thumb to match it. She also had the help of her daughters and Trainer, a full-time gardener, who tended to the grounds. The results were extraordinary. There was simply no comparison between the gardens at Dunchattan and those I remember at the three homes I lived in while I was growing up. Planted with a large variety of flowers and bushes, tended to with loving and constant care, blessed with a moist, temperate environment, the gardens at Dunchattan matched any I have tended or walked through anywhere. Interestingly enough, I had the same impression when Chloe and I visited Casa do Cerro, Alison and Jeremy's retirement home in the Algarve on the coast of Portugal, six years ago. The gardens there were not quite as lush but they were varied and beautiful, a tribute to Alison and Jeremy's prowess as gardeners. They say that the English are some of the world's finest gardeners and I would agree. I'd add, as well, that there must be a green gene in the Martin family's DNA.

Dunchattan was our headquarters in Troon but it was not the only act in town. Troon is also home to the Royal Troon Golf Club. This venerable institution, founded in 1878, has three courses, the most famous of which is the "Old Course." It is on the British Open championship rota and, at the time we walked it, boasted a 600-yard par five, the longest hole in British golf. It was dark and drizzly when I walked down the fairway of the first hole of the Old Course with Douglas. It was late in the day, windy, not a time for playing golf. But in my mind, I could picture the pleasure I'd have whacking a drive 200 yards straight down the middle of that fairway. Trouble was, as I discovered in years following, hitting a golf ball down the middle of anything was not something I did well. I had a slice, a deficiency I was never able to rectify. And with the Firth of Clyde on my right as we walked towards the pin, it is clear where my ball would have landed. Right in the Clyde.

The Lake District

Rested and refreshed after two days of Auntie Anne's TLC, we finished off a hardy Scottish breakfast of scrambled eggs and smoked salmon, gave her and Douglas a hug goodbye and hit the road. Where to? To Carlisle, just over the Scottish-English border, south of Hadrian's Wall, at the northern edge of the Lake District. Mom and Dad had motored north to Glasgow through the Lake District in 1934 and had been captivated by its beauty. Small wonder then that Dad wanted Dave and me to cycle through this region. It was eye-popping! The colorful, rolling hills and mountains, called fells here, not braes and bens, tempted us to climb them. The lakes and ponds, known as meres, tarns and waters, were glorious. Lake Windermere, Beacon Tarns, Coniston Waters, some mirrorlike, some with breezes dancing over their surfaces, beckoned us to get off our bikes, to take a swim or jump into one of the colorful boats available for rental. The half-timbered houses and colorful storefronts in quaint villages like Ambleside, Kendal and Keswick were amazing. Stop for a chat, take a picture, have a bite, buy a souvenir, why not. Sometimes we did. Nothing big, nothing expensive. We were men on the move but we were captivated. We loved the Lake District, just as Mom and Dad did, and stayed a day longer than we had planned, the first night in Penrith, the second in Kendal.

Regrettably, since Dave and I left the Lake District I never returned. But I did come close. Remembering its beauty, the warmth of its people and motivated by the possibility of making money while doing good, I invested in a green project that was being developed there by Hiram "Tony" Bingham, a college friend of mine. The project, as he described it during a cruise we took in 2006, involved the creation of a liquified natural gas storage facility, located in caves near the seacoast in the Lake District. A case for increasing the use of natural gas to replace coal for power production was gaining traction as U.K. residents began to accept the importance of going green. The U.K. still has significant resources of oil in the North Sea but, importing LNG appeared to be a viable alternative. And where to store it? The caves in the Lake District? The company to which Tony's group of investors was linked appeared to have the technical expertise to build and operate this kind of facility and the political contacts to see the project through the regulatory steps needed to initiate construction. The idea of investing in an endeavor that provided environmental benefits appealed to me, the returns being promised were attractive, and the thought of returning to the Lake District to see it in operation added an element of nostalgia.

Standing in the stern of the ocean liner on which we were traveling, watching its wake, dreaming of making a bundle while making a difference, I succumbed to the dreams of another romantic like me. Tony, the son of Hiram Bingham, the discoverer of Machu Picchu, was a dreamer just like his dad and honestly believed in the Davenport British Gas Storage project he was describing to me. I was all in after he described it to me, sold on its efficacy, eager to see his dream come true and looking forward to returning to see it evolve. Sad to say, this reason for coming back is gone. The gas storage project is dead, victim to the environmental concerns expressed by local councils.

Cycling Down the Spine of Great Britain

Memories of the route Dave and I took from the Lake District to London are dimmer than those I have of our tour of the Highlands. With the help of a map and Google searches, however, I'm amazed how memories floated into view and how reliable an image of our route emerged.

York, Lincoln and Cambridge, the cities we visited, were chosen as logical waypoints because there were hostels in them and because the distances between them were doable. In toto, we cycled a close to another 500 miles through English countryside. There was rain at times but nothing torrential and, surprisingly, we had hardly any breakdowns. Our route was mostly flat. There were some hills to climb as we rode out of the Lake District but not many thereafter as we passed though the Yorkshire Dales and cycled the 100-mile stretch between Kendal and York.

The next leg, about 75 miles in length, from York to Lincoln took us through pastoral countryside and English market towns like Crowle, Gainsborough, a charming old town on the River Trent, and Howden, once known for its horse fair. The following day we managed to go another 75-80 miles from Lincoln to Cambridge. The route we chose took us through towns like Sleaford, which once was a major player in the wool trade, Bourne, which has a rich history, culture and abundant wildlife, and Peterborough, a city of historical importance but a reputation in the U.K. today, for being one of the worst places to live. Just to the south of Peterborough lies the town of Stilton. I don't think we passed through it but our proximity to the place where Stilton cheese is made makes my mouth water as I write this sentence. I had no idea of what Stilton cheese was or tasted like when Dave and I came close to this cheese lover's mecca. But I do now and if you like a blue, cow cheese, I can tell you, there is nothing better than Stilton.

Cycling from Cambridge to London was our next challenge. This leg was just over 60 miles, shorter than most of our daily rides but, even in 1952, traffic was building and cyclists needed to be careful. Our ride that day was through a number of smallish towns, like Royston, home to around 15,00 people, a community of situated on the Greenwich Meridian, Buntingford, a stopover on what was once the main route between Cambridge and London, and Ware, sited on the picturesque River Lea, famous for its 18th Century gazebos and Scott's Grotto, built for the poet John Scott. We stopped for lunch in Buntingford but otherwise, kept pedaling until we reached our hostel in London.

During this stretch, from Troon to London we had some expected challenges but no disasters. We had a few flats. That was to be expected and we had the kit to repair them. But there were no major mechanical failures that might have affected our progress. We had more than just a bit of rain, a situation we had been told to expect, but no downpours. We had aches and pains but were able to work them out pedaling and massaging our legs with ointments, like J&J's Bengay. We had no major illnesses, accidents or other distractions that might have upset the apple cart. We were prepared, we were resourceful, and we were lucky, two young Yanks who people seemed to want to help.

When you are welcomed like we were along the way, you want to come back. The same is true of our stay in London. This city has so many wonderful things to see and do, yet the most memorable thing about it, for us, were the people we met. There were two in particular.

Sir Edward Rayne, just Edward when we visited him, was one. He had a twinkle in his eye when we walked into his office, an unexpected greeting from someone we assumed had agreed to be a surrogate chaperone. His firm's relationship with ours and his friendship with Dad had just begun but it is clear, as I reflect on that visit, that they had something in common – good taste in fashion and a good sense of fun. Edward, as we and the world would find out, was a showman, just like my father. Both knew how to get people to stand up and take notice, Edward with his couture footwear, Dad with his colorful line of fashion leathers. Both men inherited successful companies and both needed to take risks and make changes in order to keep them from becoming stale.

When we met Edward Rayne in 1952, he was just at the beginning of his long and successful reign as chairman of H. & M. Rayne. Taking over after his father's death, just months earlier, he was already on his way to instituting changes in design and merchandising, departures from his father's business model that he felt were necessary to attract customers who were looking for the type of couture footwear he intended to make. Over the years, he achieved that goal and then some, making shoes for the likes of Elizabeth Taylor, Brigitte Bardot, Marlene Dietrich and being awarded, among other things, a royal warrant that allowed his firm to supply footwear to the queen mother, the queen and other female members of the royal family.

Edward had been eyeing my father and my dad had been eyeing Edward. The time had come for Loewenstein to sell its fashion leathers in Europe. The time had also come for H. & M. Rayne to market its shoes in the U.S. This started to happen shortly after our visit when we began selling sizable quantities of leather in the U.K. to Rayne, in France to Roger Vivier and in Switzerland to Bally. We were on our way, and so was Edward, establishing an important link with the Delman brand and starting to import and sell his shoes in America.

Our lunch with Edward Rayne ended on an unexpected high note. As we got up from table at his club, he handed us an envelope containing two tickets to a show at the Windmill Theatre in Soho. This well-established London institution, founded in 1901 as a silent film theatre, the Palais de Luxe, was known as a variety and revue theatre doing burlesque. There were comedy acts to lighten the mood, but it was best known for its tableaux vivants, still, statuesque, scantily clad beauties, frozen in a variety of poses, positioned artistically on an elaborately decorated stage. Feeding the male libido was what these shows were meant to do "nudely but not rudely." I've never given too much thought as to whether buying these tickets for us was Edward's idea, but as I finish writing this paragraph, I'm beginning to wonder. Was this another oblique attempt by Dad to prepare me for the future?

Frederick Simon was the second person in London Dad wanted us to meet. He was an old friend, of my father's and my grandfather's, a German Jew who had narrowly escaped Hitler's jaws and was now an English citizen. We visited him the next morning in the London offices of Alfred Booth & Co. in South Kensington at 6 Grenville St. Friedel, as he asked us to call him, was the export manager of this venerable, far-flung English leather tanning and trading enterprise. Among many other entities, the firm owned Surpass Leather Company, a kidskin tannery in Philadelphia for which Loewenstein acted as a sales representative. Friedel visited this mill annually, and over the years, he and Dad became close friends. He became family as well, after a while, a person Dad felt we could turn to in the event of trouble and someone we could talk with about how best to spend our time in London. With but a few hours left before we were due to cycle south to spend the night with him, he came up with an excellent suggestion: take the tube and go to Buckingham Palace to see the Changing of the Guard ceremony. We did and thoroughly enjoyed these few hours of sightseeing. The pomp and circumstance was like nothing we'd ever seen, and the experience of riding a Circle Line train on the London Underground, that too was an important first for us. It was time well spent and enjoyed.

Our trip was almost finished when Dave and I cycled out to Surrey to stay overnight with Friedel and Lisl Simon at their home in Merstham. Our stay with the Simons was a one-nighter, an early dinner and then to bed. Details about the house, the dinner and the room we slept in are fuzzy, but I will not be leading anyone astray if I say that the food, the comfort and the privacy we were allowed that night were a most welcome change from our youth hostel regimen.

We were well rested when we got up early the next morning and said our goodbyes to the Simons. We had one more bit of cycling to do, from Merstham to Portsmouth, a distance of approximately 75 miles, and then a hop, by ferry, to the Isle of Wight. We had looked at the ferry schedules with Friedel the prior evening and decided to try to catch the one that left Portsmouth in the late afternoon. Today there is a boat that leaves at 5 P.M. My guess is that there was one that departed at about the same time when we were there. That meant we had to hustle and could not afford wasting any time stopping for lunch. Aware that this might be the case, Lisl had prepared sandwiches. What a blessing that was! While food was not the first thing on our minds at that time, the picnic she had prepared was tasty, nutritious and full of TLC.

Dad had insisted that we wind up our trip on the Isle of Wight. Given his love of yachting, I guess I should not have been too surprised. It is still the epicenter of yachting in the U.K, boasting 10 active yacht and sailing clubs and a history in the annals of long-distance yacht racing, unparalleled anywhere in the world. Dad had earned his stripes in this rarefied, stratified world. He had competed and won some prestigious long-distance races on Long Island Sound with his beloved ketch, Surabaya. He was still racing on the Sound and had dreams of entering the New York Yacht Club's Newport to Bermuda race. Three years later, in the summer of 1955, aboard his 56-foot yawl, Tomahawk, he actually did enter that race and finished in the top five in his class. He had nothing to be ashamed of, but there was something about the Isle of Wight that I sense kept him from setting foot on it. Was it a fear, perhaps, that he might not be accepted, as was the case when his application for membership to the Manhasset Bay Yacht Cub was blackballed, back in the early 1940s when his name was Rudolph Correll Loewenstein? We never talked about this snub, but I am sure it must have had its effect on him.

Besides yacht and sailing clubs, there were lots of piers, boardwalks and beaches on the Isle of Wight. If we wanted to switch from bikes to another sort of ride, Blackgang Chine, the oldest amusement park in the U.K., was operating when we arrived. Appealing? Perhaps, but I doubt we chose to go to see it and buy tickets for some of its rides. We had a just a few hours that evening and then a day, tomorrow, before we had to leave the Isle of Wight to board our boat back home in Southampton. There were better things to do than visiting amusement parks, weren't there? How about a bike ride around the perimeter of the island, a bit of exploring? Or maybe a few hours soaking up some sun on one of the beaches? If the choice I have in mind today mirrors our decision back then, the beach would have been where we headed. In the meantime we had a few hours to kill, after our ferry pulled into the ferry pier at Fishbourne. I have little doubt that after checking into our hostel, we would not have found a place to have a beer, a light meal, something like fish and chips, and then head off, not to bed, but to one of the boardwalks to do some last-minute cruising.

Arriving in Southampton the next morning we cycled from the ferry dock to the pier where we would be boarding our ship later that morning. We had boarding tickets. We knew that we would not be going home on a freighter but not much more, about the vessel or the amenities on board. We were about to find out and we did, shortly after we boarded the MS Ryndam, but there is still much for me to discover as I try to reconstruct our two ocean voyages.

Filling in the blanks on our voyages to and from the U.K. has become an interesting, ongoing exercise. My memory regarding the shipping lines we traveled on, checked out. Going over from Baltimore, we sailed aboard an Anchor Line freighter. Coming back, we took a small Holland-America ocean liner from Southampton to New York. I even found a picture of an Anchor Line freighter on the internet. Getting a shipping manifest remains a work in progress, a challenge, a sweet victory if one can be found, but not a necessity.

The same is true about pinpointing the vessel on which we sailed home. Here I had better luck. The research I did concerning shipping lines with liners that sailed the Southampton-New York route indicated that Holland-America had a number of ocean liners sailing that route. A search of the ships they've operated over the years provided a listing of the liners in operation in 1952. Relying on my memory that the ship we sailed on was much smaller than the Queen Mary Dad and Mom once took to Southampton, I narrowed the choices down to one ship, the MS Ryndam. Once again, the search goes on for a manifest and, if one is found, a cork will be popped.

So back to my story about our return trip to the U.S. aboard the Ryndam. I have little doubt that we traveled in anything better than tourist class. I have no idea whether we were in an outside or inside cabin, but I would guess the latter. Wherever we may have been placed, our quarters were certainly more spacious and attractive than those we slept in on the trip over. I don't remember much about dining or dress code, but I'm sure the cuisine was several cuts above what we had on our freighter and that Holland-America did not even require a sports jacket and tie at dinnertime. There was entertainment aboard, movies, shows, dancing. I'm sure I sampled some of these amenities but, as I started thinking about returning to Lawrenceville, I'm sure that my biggest concern was staying fit. There was a fitness room aboard in the bow of the liner, which I used regularly. Within days of our return, I would be headed back to Lawrenceville for preseason football practice and I wanted to be in shape. My legs were good and strong but I needed to do some weight training. This I did, faithfully,

And there was a girl, as you might have expected, Lindsay Findlay, a pretty young thing who was traveling with her parents. There was nothing special about her, no shipboard romance or anything even close. But I did dance with her once or twice, and having a girl in my arms felt nice. In later life, she reappeared twice, at Goucher, while Chloe was a student there and, in the 1990s, at the Columbia Business School, where I was trying my hand at teaching, assisting an adjunct professor whose class, "The Joy of Running Your Own Business," was immensely popular. Ironic, isn't it, that Lindsay would have first met me when I was being prepared to run my own business and reappeared years later, when I was helping teach that course about running your own business.

Our summer across the pond ended when Dave and I got off the Ryndam in New York. Mom and Dad were there to greet me. So were Dave's parents. Welcoming hugs were followed by lunch at a restaurant on the West Side. All were anxious to hear our stories. Question followed question. Dave and I had certainly learned something, and not just about leather tanning. We had grown a lot during this trip and learned a lot, about the world and about ourselves. No question, whether Dad thought about it in this way or not, our summer across the pond had been a rite of passage. There would be much to think and talk about as we put the lessons we'd learned to good use. The formal education I had gotten and would get in future years would serve me well. But this trip had taught me something equally, if not more important: how to live, successfully and safely, in the real world.

The places Dave and I visited that summer are still there and I have come back to many of them. Many of the people I got to know during that journey have since passed away but most of the relationships I formed did not fade away. I treasure the ones I still have and do my best to keep them vibrant. That said, before I bring this chapter of my life to a close, I'd like to tell you what happened afterwards. It's a story within a story worth telling. Here below, are some updates, of the places I returned to and the people that played such significant roles, during the course of this trip and the rest of my life.

Places We Visited

Many of the sights in the Highlands that Dave and I saw in 1952 I was destined to see again. When Chloe and I took a cruise up the Caledonian Canal with our friends Bob and Karen Brown in 2005, we traveled in comfort on the elegant hotel barge, the Spirit of Scotland. That mode of luxurious transport certainly provided a quite different perspective from the one I had formed on my cycling trip with Dave. The cabins and public rooms on this vessel were plush, service was attentive, meals were of gourmet quality and sightseeing was a daily, intriguing diversion. We toured castles and gardens. We tromped over battlefields and plunged deeply into Scottish history. We searched for Nessie with gusto but again, without success. And we sampled single malt Scotch whiskies, from various regions of the Highlands with pleasure and discernment. That trip, lovely and luxurious as it was, reinforced rather than erased the experience Dave and I had when I first encountered the haunting beauty of this magic part of the world.

Another reason for going back to Scotland was to visit our dear friends, Bill and Brenda Martin. They returned to Scotland in 1993 when Bill decided to retire and not long thereafter, we resumed our friendship, face to face, visiting them in their new home in Avoch on the Black Isle. Over the years, we extended our "long weekend" trips to London many times, flying EasyJet to Inverness in order to spend several extra days with them, first at the home they built on a hill in Avoch and later on in their slightly smaller abode in Fortrose. What joy we had walking through their lovely gardens, camping out in their living room at Bishops Wood and having wee "natters" as we drank a refreshing cup of tea or took a nip of single malt. Remembering the view from that room, looking down on the little harbor below always brings me inner peace. It's like coming home to family to be with them, a return to a spot in this world I've grown to love, and to the beginning of a relationship that began 70 years ago.

Chloe and I have also enjoyed visiting York and Cambridge. In York, we rented an apartment with Bill and Brenda in an unusual venue they discovered, a three-room flat in what had once been a brewery. Surprisingly, it proved to be an ideal spot, comfy and cozy, within walking distance of the places Bill wanted us to see. I did not know what to expect. York was just a way point when Dave and I spent a night there. This time was completely different. Our days in York became special, an opportunity for reconnecting with the two of them, for strolling down cobblestone streets, being serenaded by buskers, window shopping and sampling local fare in attractive bistros and restaurants. I am not a history buff, but I got a real sense of the city and its history during an entertaining trolley ride at the Jorvik Viking Centre. It really made the city's history come alive. Another attraction was the National Railway Museum. I love trains, real ones and model trains. And there were plenty of them to see and board in this rather amazing museum, an unexpected plus.

I returned to Cambridge as well, with Chloe in 2012, as part of a group Yale alumni, aka YaleGale, that would be visiting several British universities to spread the word about what the AYA, the Association of Yale Alumni was doing for and with Yale alums. YaleGale, an acronym for Yale Graduate Alumni Leadership Exchange, was an interesting idea, initiated by Mark Dollhopf, head of the AYA at the time. Mark worked diligently to build a strong connection with alumni through established regional Yale groups and clubs, alumni with similar interests (SIGs), and outreach efforts like the Yale Day of Service which encouraged alumni to "give back" to their communities in a positive way, by performing some meaningful service that would make a difference in the quality of life in their communities. YaleGale's membership was comprised of alumni active in one or more of these programs and trips such as the one, were meant to inspire universities abroad to build alumni organizations similar to Yale's. YaleGale no longer exists, but it was a good idea and Mark was able to organize several trips, to Australia, Turkey, China, Israel, the UK and Mexico. YaleGale, I'm told, was welcomed on all these excursions. I remember vividly the treatment we got on our trip to the UK where host universities in Edinburgh, Liverpool, Cambridge and London. Cambridge, rolled out the red carpet for us. Dave and I were certainly well received by the folks we met in London in 1952 but the amenities tendered to our YaleGale group when we visited were, quite understandably, many cuts above what was offered to young Yanks like us. For example, a reception at Christ College was organized for YaleGale where we shared our vision of what alumni associations might look like and do. Another treat was the vespers service we attended in the chapel at Kings College. A walk along the River Cam in Cambridge was equally pleasurable. There's nothing like seeing university students at play, some punting in its slow flowing water, others frolicking on its banks. Most memorable for me though, was the time we spent touring the American Cemetery and World War II Memorial, in Cambridge, where we saw the extensive number of white marble headstones, massed together, row upon row, flanked by a reflecting pool, at the end of which stood the high ceilinged, stone columned, memorial building. It was hard not to feel sadness, and pride, as I viewed this tribute to the men who gave their lives to protect our freedom during that war.

Besides business reasons for being there, London has always been number one on my list of places to go for a pleasant holiday. I've returned there many, many times with Chloe, with friends and sometimes with family. Theater was always one of the big draws. Broadway was much closer to home but, spurred on by our friends David and Ellen Freeman, I dare say we saw more shows in the West End, the Globe and the National Theater than we ever did on the Great White Way. The precipitating factor for travel to London was invariably, a discounted airline fare. When David spotted one, he would email us this news plus a list of shows he thought would be fun to see and special museum exhibitions we might want to view. Once digested, this information led quickly to the booking of air and theater tickets and hotel rooms. The next step was reserving a table at Gordon Ramsay's restaurant on the Royal Hospital Road. Tables go quickly at this elegant restaurant and timing is everything. Reservations are taken 90 days in advance and emails to secure a table that are sent later than noon that day are likely to miss the mark. Over the years, having lunch there became a tradition and David made sure that never happened, getting up at six in the morning to call or send an email.

His early morning heroics successful, we could rest easy and look forward to a special treat, an extraordinary five-course lunch. From the savory "amuse bouche" that started us off, to the decadent chocolate morsels accompanying our after-dinner expressos, these meals were truly memorable. The combination of delicious food, outstanding service and tasteful, understated décor was hard to beat and we didn't try. We became regulars, always welcomed with ceremony by its maître d', a charming young Frenchman who always made sure that we were well taken care. The price tag for these lunches is equally memorable but being treated like royalty is something special, a reason for returning.

Well-fed and entertained, we sought to fill the rest of our time with other activities, like shopping excursions to Harrods, buying toys for the kids at Hamleys or visiting one or more of the many museums and other tourist attractions in London.

I've been very lucky. Having the resources, health and reasons, both personal and business, I've been able to indulge my wanderlust and visit some of the world's most attractive, exciting cities and countries. Travel has its challenges, but, by and large, the trips I've taken in my lifetime have been enriching, entertaining and eye-opening. Theater, music, restaurants, museums, sports venues, amusements and history. London has them all and that is why I've returned so many, many times. These are the attractions one normally looks for when planning a trip and all are important. But one thing is missing from that list. For me the most important thing when I plan a trip is the people. Who do I know in the countries, states, cities and towns I hope to visit? If I have friends there, I call them to see if we can meet. If I know someone who has family or friends there, I try to contact them. If none of the above is possible and I didn't speak the language, I would buy a set of Pimsleur tapes or a phrasebook so I could utter a few basic phrases. Not everyone feels that way, but it's the people, talking with them, understanding them and making friends with them that makes trips to foreign lands so meaningful, enjoyable and memorable.

People

First and foremost, I want to profile my friend and cycling partner Dave Strite. Dave entered Bucknell when we got back and shortly thereafter broke up with his girlfriend Jeanette Kullak. With that bond broken, our close friendship started to whither and when I moved to Plandome Manor and went off to Yale, we hardly saw one another. The last time we did was just before he joined the Army and was sent to Monterey, California to learn Russian. We spoke once or twice while he was there, but I completely lost contact with him when he was assigned to a listening post in the Aleutian Islands. Many years later, our paths crossed again, in Santa Fe, where Dave and his wife Carol had retired. The occasion was a mini reunion in 2010 that my Yale class of 1957 was staging. We had never connected with them in the 50-plus intervening years, but having learned from a mutual friend that Dave and Carol were living there , we asked him to reach out to see if they would be interested in seeing us. The answer was an enthusiastic yes. And when we met it was like we had never been separated. There was so much to talk about, so much to do. Meeting and getting to know Carol, filling in blanks – what had happened in our lives in those years we hadn't seen each other. . We took another trip to Santa Fe a few years later, just to see Carol and Dave. We maintained ties from that point forward and they planned to come to see us as well in Johnstown. Unfortunately, that never happened

Dave, sadly, is no longer with us. He died in 2016. But I've kept in touch with Carol who helped refresh my memory on the details of their lives in the 50 years Dave and I lived miles apart. Turns out Dave and I married in the same year, 1957, Dave to Carol, nee Keator, I to Chloe, nee Anderson. Neither of us were groomsmen or attended each other's weddings, something I regret in retrospect. We each had kids. Dave had two, David and James. I had three, Cathy, Douglas and Edward. We both had long careers in the industry we first set foot in. Dave's work for Corn Products, Kraft and Tupperware involved posts in Argentina, Chile, Uruguay and Switzerland. I wound up becoming a successful leader of a small, privately held company and wonder what it must have been like for Dave climbing the ladder in large, multinational ones. I envy him the diversity of his geographical postings. I would have loved to live abroad for a few years, learning a different language, making a new set of friends, attuned to a different culture and cuisine. Living abroad must certainly have been challenging, but rewarding as well for Dave and his family.

Bill Martin is the next person up to bat on my list of best friends. Bill has been an omnipresent feature in my life, ever since we met in 1952. The multifaceted business relationship I've had with him over the years has blossomed into one of the closest, most cherished friendships, with him and his family, that I am blessed to have. In business, Bill has played for me the roles of mentor, supplier, employee and successor. Socially, he, his wife Brenda and daughters Erica, Corrine and Carola have become as much members of our family as anyone with whom we have relationships. I owe so much to Bill. As I transitioned out of my family's firm and the leather industry, I needed help, both tactically and emotionally. Without his willingness to assist me in this move forward, the positive change in my life's path might never have happened. In addition, both Chloe and I have so much for which to thank both Brenda and Bill. They gave us loving counsel and support as we delt with the challenges of being parents to a brilliant but disruptive child, a sorely needed gift. They came through for us over many years, and our entire family has benefitted from the many kindnesses extended by various members of the Martin clan. This started when they moved stateside but has continued for many years, during the time they were living in the U.S. and thereafter, when they went back to their native Scotland. They and their family epitomize what friendship should mean and be.

Dave and Bill are my peers, men I befriended before and during my 1952 odyssey. Douglas and Anne Martin played roles as surrogate parents, a totally different but equally important relationship, in 1952 and afterwards. Uncle Dougal and Auntie Anne, the names by which I will forever remember them, passed away many years ago, but not before Chloe and I visited them in Dunchattan shortly after we were married. On that memorable visit, Auntie Anne, served us poached salmon, caught by none other than, you guessed it, Auntie Anne. And where did she catch that fish? In the River Dee, of course, but this time there was no queen to watch her. Quite naturally, however, her story about curtseying to Queen Elizabeth was retold, with a flourish, as she served her salmon to us. And that was not the end of the salmon stories. A new one was in store for us. There was more salmon, PMIK, "plenty more in kitchen." In this particular case, besides the leftovers which were on the table there was, indeed, another fish in the freezer. This one she suggested we take home, in frozen form, when we returned to the U.S. the following morning. With Prestwick, Glasgow's international airport, just five miles away, this caper, as outlandish as it might seem today, appeared doable.

And what could be more enticing than smuggling this delectable three-pound delicacy past U.S. Customs? Not much so an ingenious plan was hatched. The frozen salmon, covered with a layer of clear cling wrap, would be taken out of the freezer, just prior to our departure for the airport and stuffed into a long paper bag, the kind used to carry baguettes home from a bakery. Matching it, in length and packaging, was a decoy, a baguette bag into which we inserted the roly-poly, flowered fabric dachshund doll we had bought for our daughter at Liberty's of London. These two packages would be put into a tote bag that we would carry with us onto the airplane and, once in our seats, call our stewardess requesting that she put our salmon stuffed baguette bag in the plane's refrigerator. Our stewardess was lovely and as mischievous as we had become. The salmon found a new home in the fridge for the rest of the flight and was handed back to us, just before deplaning.

So far so good. Upon landing at Idlewild, we deplaned with the tote bag in hand and collected our luggage at the baggage carousel. With our bags placed on a luggage cart and the tote bag resting on top of them, we headed to one of the customs kiosks. We presented our customs declaration form and, when he asked what was in our tote bag, we pulled out our decoy, the baguette bag with our dachshund it. As we did so we mused about how happy our daughter would be when she got that dog and its brother in the other baguette bag. In today's world we would never have gotten away with this sort of a boondoggle but in 1960, well before 9/11, we managed to so. And boy, did that fish taste good!

We saw the Martin daughters as well in late years. Anne, the oldest, was married by the time Chloe and I paid our visit to Dunchattan and became a friend over the years. Her husband, Dennis Williams, had taken over as sales manager at W&JM by that time. He was well suited of the job, a superb salesman, a gregarious back slapper, a genial host. I remember fondly visiting them and, their three children, Douglas, Anne and Martin, at their home in Edinburgh when we came to Scotland with our daughter Cathy in the mid-60's. I can still can envision the eight of us doing a Highland jig, hand in hand, on their lawn, overlooking the city of Edinburgh. It was a joyous moment and is a vivid memory. The middle daughter, Agnes Mary, whom we met in the summer of 1952, was married later that year to John Yencken, an Australian entrepreneur, if memory serves, who whisked her away, shortly after their wedding, to his native land. I never corresponded or saw her again, but Douglas kept Dad well informed of what was happening Down Under in that branch of the Martin family.

I talked earlier of Alison's visit to the U.S. We had sporadic correspondence since that trip and reconnected when many years later when Chloe and I took a trip to Portugal in 2016. In preparing for that trip, I reached out to Alison to see if we might not visit her and Jeremy in their new home in the Algarve. Her answer was a hearty yes. And, what fun we had, being with them at Casa do Cerro, enjoying their lovely home and gardens, sight-seeing with them nearby and then driving on to Seville. We had visited them previously, at their home in Surrey, when Jeremy was still working in London. The gardens they had created there were lush, large, colorful, manicured and varied, a work of art. Fast forward now, from the temperate, moist climate of Great Britain to the warmer drier one in the Algarve. Add a few years in age and a few more aches and pains. And what do you get? Another exceptional garden, smaller, less varied, but equally beautiful.

Another character who played a significant role during our visit to London in 1952 faded out of the picture for me, and for my dad, not long after our visit to his office. Business reasons for being in London were on an uptick when I joined the firm. Dad had kept up with Edward Rayne during the years I was in college, but sales to his firm had dropped off by the time I started working at Loewenstein. Our connection to H. & M.

Rayne continued but was now kept alive through a friendship our fashion director, Nancy Shapiro, had with Jean Matthew, one of Rayne's top shoe designers. It was Jean who designed the shoes that Rayne made for Princess Margaret when she married Anthony Armstrong-Jones, a pair of elegant triple-needle toe high heels, made out of Loewenstein's Peppermint Pink Gamuza Suede. When I reorganized Loewenstein in 1971 and Chloe took over as my fashion consultant, she got news of the fashion story in London. A close friendship developed and we started to see Jean whenever we came to London. Lunch in the roof restaurant at the National Portrait Gallery was the usual arrangement, but once, I still vividly remember, we treated her to high tea at the Ritz. That was special. So were the specialty cards she frequently made and gave to her friends. I have one of these on my desk as I type these lines. I smile every time I look at it.

I saw Friedel Simon several times in the years after we met in 1952. He traveled to the U.S. annually and would stop at Dad's office on Ferry Street when he was in New York. He also came out to Mom and Dad's house quite often for dinner. I would meet him there when I was home from college and, from 1957 onward, I'd see him annually in Paris at the Semaine du Cuir. This international leather fair was held in September. Dad always encouraged me to walk the show and see what was going on. Besides tanneries with a broad array of leathers on display, there were stands set up by companies serving the leather industry; machine makers, chemical producers, hide and skin dealers, fashion services, media and more. There was much to see and many people to schmooze with – our customers, our suppliers and occasionally a friendly competitor. At some point in my walk-arounds, I would stop at the Booth & Co. stand. If he was not busy, I would share my impressions with Friedel. He would come over to the Loewenstein booth as well to talk with Dad. Dad had a favorite restaurant nearby, a peniche (river barge) docked on the Seine near the exhibition hall at the Porte de Versailles. If Dad wasn't working with an important customer, they would slip away for lunch. If I was lucky, I'd be invited along. Those were happy days!

Besides those lunches, there were dinners, some rather elaborate. I remember best one at the Hotel Bristol to which Dad, Chloe and I were invited. It was hosted by Booth & Co. during the 1962 Semaine du Cuir. When Dad came to Paris for this exhibition and trade fair, he would always stay at the Bristol. It wasn't the Ritz, but it was a very toney second best. Its restaurant was very good, not five-star Michelin quality but up there in terms of menu and service. Boasting a private dining room that could seat 30 people, it was an ideal venue for the kind of party Booth was throwing for its far-flung corporate family. Chloe and I felt a bit awed being included in this upscale affair, but with Friedel sitting between us, we managed to hold our own. It's hard to say exactly the role he played in my life. Teacher is a good description. And role model; that may be the best way to describe Freidel. In writing this book I've learned a few lessons, including how Friedel helped me. My Dad opened the door to learning about the leather business, Freidel helped me connect the dots.

SCENE 2:

Kidskin Tanning in Offenbach am Main – 1954

My first visit to Offenbach occurred in 1953, during my tour of Europe with my Lawrenceville roommates, Clarence "Ren" Zimmerman and Peter Balbach. The following year, Dad arranged a one month stay for me at the J. Mayer & Sohn tannery. Job No. 1 while I was there was to meet the people and learn how they did things. Job No. 2 was to get a good understanding of the leather they were making. And Job No. 3, a personal challenge, was to become more fluent in German. Being in Offenbach was a real learning and, in the process, friend-making experience. There were many people I got to know there during that summer but one, in particular, stands out, Walter Schneider, the guy who would ultimately work with me building Mayer's sales in the United States. We bonded in the month I spent in training in Offenbach. It wasn't all work either. Walter knew German wines quite well and introduced me to a variety of them at local wine fests. He loved good, simple food and delighted in my reaction to the name of the German hamburger, frikadellen, and in my relish for spargels. These wonderful fat, white asparagus were one of my mother's favorites, a delicacy Germans feast on when they are harvested, from mid-April to the end of June. Another memory, a favorite of mine, had nothing to do with wine, food or leather. It was the day Walter took me to a toy store to look at model trains. I was quickly hooked and bought a starter set of HO gauge Marklin trains. I'd always loved playing with Dad's O gauge Lionel trains and couldn't resist the temptation of building my own little empire. Compared to the cost of Dad's Lionels and what I would have to pay for Marklins in the U.S., this set was a bargain. So why not? I took the plunge and, a few years later, I started building that empire. As sales of the Mayer & Sohn line grew and I became its sales manager, I became a smuggler. Perusing the Marklin catalog, I would identify items I wanted. After checking what we had in the bank and getting a green light from Chloe, I would send Walter orders for engines, rolling stock, track, transformers and plastic bridge and station kits. The works! He would buy these items for me, judiciously tuck them into selected cartons of leather and then inform me into which cartons he had packed my little gems. Our somewhat nefarious scheme worked smoothly over the three years it took for me to become a model railroad baron.

My little fiefdom was impressive. It was nowhere near as elaborate as Dad's, but my kids loved it. Working with wire mesh and plaster of Paris, Dad had created a mountain through which his trains ran. The highlight of an evening of model train high jinks on Dad's layout always came when one of his trains emerged from the tunnel in his mountain. Why? Perhaps because there was some doubt that, once in the tunnel, we would never see that train again? Unlikely? Well, one day it didn't emerge by itself. And why was that? It just so happened that "Woody Herman," a white lab rat, a so-called pet, brought home from a birthday party by my sister Lenie, had decided to camp out in the tunnel. Once the problem was diagnosed, it was quickly solved; the train was extracted manually, Woody was flushed out of his comfy lair, and a new home was found for him. The track inside the tunnel was pulled out and cleaned and, danke schön, the trains started running on time again. The Woody Herman saga has nothing whatsoever to do with my learning to be a leatherman. In retrospect, however, I'll hypothesize that it was obliquely connected, an example of the organized way Dad reacted when he faced a problem.

PEOPLE

PEOPLE

The Correll Family

THREE GENERATIONS OF LOEWENSTEIN LEADERS

My grandfather, my father and I were quite different in personality and the way we ran the family business. Our challenges were markedly so, but there was one thing we all did. The three of us inspired confidence in our ability to deliver quality product, at a fair price, on time.

ACAPULCO VACATION

We didn't go on many family vacations but this one to Mexico, first to Mexico City and Cuernavaca, then on to Acapulco, was pure pleasure. Our hats mirror our smiles and spirits.

MOM AND DAD - HAPPIER DAYS

Besides riding this donkey in Portugal in 1953, Mom also rode shotgun as Dad drove Peter Rabbit, the Hillman Minx they turned over to me in London.

MY MOTHER AND HER MOTHER

[LEFT] Mom, smiling and holding one of her Chesterfields, stands on a gravel walkway at our first home in Kenilworth, a gated community in Kings Point.

[RIGHT] A portrait of Mom painted by Alexander Brooke in 1937, two years after I was born

[LEFT] A portrait of Mom painted by a Russian artist in 1953, shortly after we moved to Broadlawn Harbor.

[RIGHT] A portrait of my grandmother, whom I called Omi, painted in Germany, circa 1910.

THE KIDS

Rod

Lenie

Stevie

Judy

Four siblings: Lenie, Stevie, Judy and me in 1944

Dad, Paulette and Suzette, on the deck at their summer home on Eaton's Neck. A new, happy and vibrant branch of the Correll family.

Very Important People

Bill Martin, businessman, on the road in the 1970s

Dave Strite in California, when he lived there in the 1960s

Bill Martin, prankster, on vacation with his family on the island of Colonsay.

Douglas and Anne Martin, kitted out for salmon fishing on the River Dee in the 1950s

Douglas and Anne Martin in their garden at Dunchattan in the 1950s

Joe Vago and his daughter Marta, in Budapest, circa 1980s. Joe was my mentor as I got started at Hermann Loewenstein. Marta, who I met many years later at an FFI conference at Brigham Young University, was awarded the prestigious Certificate in Family Business Advising with Fellow Status by the Family Firm Institute in 2001 and was recipient of its 2004 International Award for promoting the understanding of family enterprise between countries.

PLACES

Family Homes

"BROADLAWN," East Shore Road, GREAT NECK, L. I.

A Splendid Long Island Estate

Now on the Market. Unusual Bargain

BROADLAWN, the estate of Angie M. Booth, 50 acres, all under cultivation, in Long Island's choicest country estate section, frontage on Manhasset Bay.   Imposing Southern Colonial homestead; 16 rooms, including 8 masters' bedrooms, 6 baths.   Servants' quarters, semi-detached, 4 rooms and baths.

Stables have space for 12 head of cattle and 10 horses; hot water heat.   Dairy of most modern type, every sanitary device; fully tiled and electrically equipped.   Ice house attached.   Service living quarters, 3 suites for families, 3 baths, 4 rooms and bath for single men, over the stables.   Separate garage accommodating 6 cars.   Chauffeur's quarters, suite of 5 rooms and bath, overhead.   Greenhouse for flowers and table vegetables.   Flower packing house with room for delivery car, and living quarters for gardeners above.   Superintendent's cottage, 6 rooms equipped with every modern convenience, hot water heat.

For immediate sale to close the estate of Angie M. Booth.   Inquiries solicited.   Inspection only by appointment.   Brokers protected.

AMERICAN TRUST COMPANY
Administrator C. T. A.
135 BROADWAY   NEW YORK
Write to the Real Estate Department for further particulars

The second home we lived in when Dad moved the family out to Kings Point, on the North Shore of Long Island. This house and grounds, a former estate, christened Broadlawn Harbor by its developer, were stuff to build a dream on.

Our third home in Plandome Manor, an old ferry depot that had been converted into a magnificent waterfront residence.

The old leather district in lower Manhattan as it was in the 1930s through the 1960s, home to the sales offices and warehouses of U.S. and foreign leather tanneries, merchants and jobbers

Sweets was an easy walk from our office at 26 Ferry St., making it the eatery of choice when out of town customers came to visit us. There was nothing fancy about the restaurant but the seafood they served was very tasty.

The 1952 Bike Trip

Pictured in Pollockshields, this is the type of tram Dave and I rode between the tannery and our hotel in that area of Glasgow.

A Raleigh three-speed English racer, the type of bike we rode.

Dave in the Scottish Highlands

Dave and I sailed home from England on the SS Ryndam in August of 1952. The cruise ship is shown the year before on her maiden voyage from Southampton to the Holland-America Line pier on the Hudson River in New York City.

With the help of memory, maps, feasibility estimates and Google searches, I assembled the data to create this spreadsheet outlining our bike route, seen on the following pages.

1952 TRIP ACROSSS THE POND

Day #	Departure Pt - Destination
1	NYC (Penn Stn) - Baltimore
2 - 13	Baltimore - Livepool
30	Liverpool - Glasgow
15 - 29	Glasgow
30	Pollockshields - Pitlochry
31	Pitlochry - Inverness
32	Inverness - Gairloch
33	Gairloch - Inverness
34	Inverness - Ft William
35	Ft Willian - Tarbet
36	Tarbet - Troon
37	Troon
38	Troon - Carlisle
39	Carlisle - Keswick
40	Lake District
41	Kendal - York
42	York - Lincoln
43	Lincoln - Cambridge
44	Cambridge - London
45	London
46	London
47	London - Merstham
48	Merstham - Isle of Wight
49	Isle of Wight
50	Isle of Wight - Southampton
51 - 59	Southampton - New York

1952 TRIP ACROSSS THE POND

Via	Conveyance	Miles
PRR Boston - Miami tracks	Pennsylvania RR	175
Atlantic Ocean	HMS Whatchamacallit	3,275
British Rail	British RR	220
W & JM Tannery	Trainee	
Dunblane, Creiff, Dunkeld	Bicycle	87
Dahlwhinnie, Kingussie	Bicycle	88
Garve, Inchabe, Dundonnell	Bicycle & Car	98
Talladale, Kinlochewe, Achnasheen	Bicycle	70
Drumnadrochit, Ft, Augustus	Bicycle	67
Glencoe, Crianlarich	Bicycle	68
Dunbarton, Paisley, Kilmarnock	Bicycle	63
at Dunchattan	At Rest	
Cumnock, Dumfries	Bicycle	97
Caldbeck, Bassenthwaite	Bicycle	33
at Kendal	Bicycle	
Ingleton, Skipton, Harrowgate	Bicycle	103
Howden, Crowle, Gainsborough	Bicycle	71
Sleaford, Bourne, Peterborough	Bicycle	76
Newport, Sansted, Epping	Bicycle	63
	At Rest	
	At Rest	
Croydon, Banstead	Bicycle	16
Guilford, Petersfield, Portsmouth	Bicycle & Ferry	68
	Cycle Tour of Isle	
Yarmouth	Bicycle & Ferry	10
Atlantic Ocean	RMS Ryndam	3,635

Lawrenceville

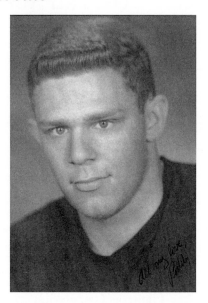

Front cover of the 1952 Olla Podrida, the Lawrenceville School yearbook.

That's me in a Lawrenceville football program.

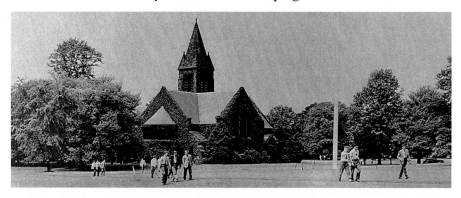

Edith Memorial Chapel at Lawrenceville where the student body assembled every weekday at noon.

Lavino Fieldhouse where I suited up for football.

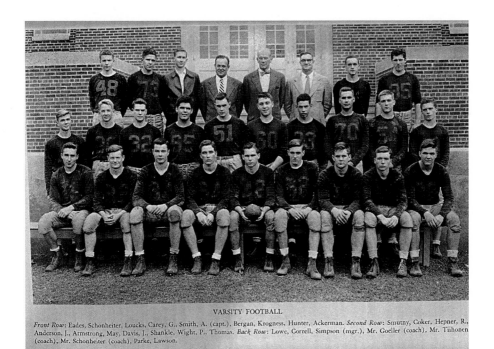

VARSITY FOOTBALL

Front Row: Eades, Schonheiter, Loucks, Carey, G., Smith, A. (capt.), Bergan, Krogness, Hunter, Ackerman. *Second Row*: Smutny, Coker, Hepner, R., Anderson, J., Armstrong, May, Davis, J., Shankle, Wight, P., Thomas. *Back Row*: Lowe, Correll, Simpson (mgr.), Mr. Goeller (coach), Mr. Tiihonen (coach), Mr. Schonheiter (coach), Parke, Lawson.

The 1952 varsity football team.

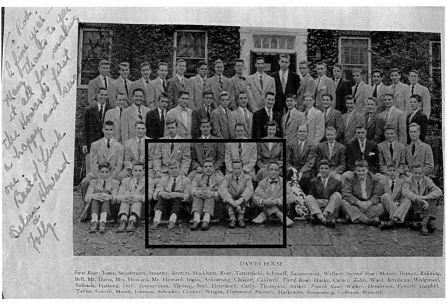

DAWES HOUSE

First Row: Jones, Steinbrunn, Smutny, Britton, Stockham, Rose, Tattersfield, Schrauff, Zimmerman, Wallace. *Second Row*: Meyers, Hepner, Rohlfing, Bell, Mr. Davis, Mrs. Howard, Mr. Howard, Inglis, Armstrong, Chilcott, Caldwell. *Third Row*: Haake, Carney, Zoble, Ward, Bernheim, Wedgwood, Balbach, Hattong, Dull, Zimmerman, Thomas, Istel, Henriksen, Carey, Thompson, Striker. *Fourth Row*: Walker, Henderson, Fawcett, Gambill, Taylor, Correll, Moore, Johnson, Schocket, Conkey, Wright, Fleetwood, Shoettle, Harkrader, Sonnenberg, Coffman, Brancart.

Residents of Dawes House, one of six dormitories housing sophomores and juniors, so called second and third formers, in 1952.

52 Olla Podrida 52

First Row: Harrah, Wright, J., McCurrach, Soper, Dole, Anderson, Wellmeier, Hammond, T., Langhorne, Correll, Harper. *Second Row*: Wight, C., Chilcott, Britton, Hutchinson, Henriksen, Orvald, Love, Snedeker, Savitz, Li, Breig. *Third Row*: Burton, Nixon, Marcus, Smith, R., Parke, Chivers, Bernheim, Dickinson, Shankle, Davis, D., Schirmer. *Fourth Row*: Carnegie, Weltner, Reading, Johnson, E., Green, B., Hartong, Gardner, Lowe, Snyder, C., Gentry. *Fifth Row*: May, Gaines, White, G., Carey, G., Fox, Goodlett, Smith, J., Smith, A., Pattison, Conger, Burt, Olsen, Twohy (absent).

THE GLEE CLUB

First Tenors

| Anderson, J. | Breig | Butman | Clarke, A. | Hammond, T. | May | Wright, J. |
| Bernheim | Burton | Carey, G. | Dole | Langhorne, J. | Orvald | |

Second Tenors

Britton	Chilcott	Hartong	Marcus	Reading	Schirmer
Burt	Dalrymple	Henriksen	Omaña, C.	Rubincam	Snedeker
Carnegie	Fox	Langhorne, E.	Pattison, M.	Savitz	White, G.

Baritones

Chivers	Gardner	Hutchinson	Nixon	Peck, T.	Snyder, C.
Cote	Goodlett	Johnson	O'Callaghan, H.	Parke, J.	
Davis, D.	Harrah	Loucks	Olsen	Shankle	

Basses

Conger	Gaines	Harper	Lowe	Null, S.	Soper	Weltner
Correll	Gentry	Hulshizer	Love	Smith, A.	Twohy	Wight, C.
Dickinson	Green, B.	Li	MacIlvaine	Smith, R.	Wellmeier	

The 1952 Lawrenceville Glee Club. I sang in this group and the choir, just as Dad had done during his three years at Lawrenceville.

Yale

Harkness Tower, a landmark on the Old Campus, home of Yale freshmen.

The entryway to my third-floor single in North Berkeley in my senior year.

Aerial view of the Yale Bowl during the Yale-Army game of 1952 in which the Bulldogs upset the Cadets, 14 – 12

[ABOVE] A well-worn wooden Yale bulldog that kept me company in my undergraduate years.

[LEFT] The Phi Gamma Delta house on Fraternity Row.

A picture of close friends at Yale and their parents celebrating our graduation in 1957.

"A Farewell to Bright College Years" was the Life magazine cover story with photos by Alfred Eisenstaedt. It told the story through the graduation experience of Roger Dennis "Denny" Hansen, one of the stars of the Class of 1957, as he said goodbye to a life that was so full of promise but ended tragically with his suicide at age 51. Tragically, as readers of Calvin Trillin's book Remembering Denny will be aware, "Denny" Hansen, then 51 and known as Dr. Roger Hansen, took his own life. Feeling hopelessly trapped, a homosexual, unable lived to "come out of the closet" in the unforgiving world in which he lived, saw no alternative to suicide. Things have changed since then, thanks to the activism of another Y57 classmate, Larry Kramer, but the battle for equal rights and the stigma felt by people who identify as LGBT remains tenuous. A sad state of affairs!

LIFE

CHIANG KAI-SHEK TELLS
OF COEXISTENCE WITH
REDS, WHY IT FAILED

EUROPEAN ROYALTY: II

FRANCO'S CANDIDATE
TO BE KING OF SPAIN

20 CENTS

JUNE 24, 1957

U.S. PAT. OFF.

Vol. 42, No. 25

REG. U.S. PAT. OFF.

June 24, 1957

© 1957 TIME INC. ALL RIGHTS RESERVED UNDER INTERNATIONAL AND PAN-AMERICAN COPYRIGHT CONVENTIONS. REPRODUCTION IN WHOLE OR PART WITHOUT WRITTEN PERMISSION IS STRICTLY PROHIBITED

Following list shows sources from which pictures were gathered. Credits are separated from left to right by commas, top to bottom by dashes.

COVER—NINA LEEN
2—HANK WALKER—YALE JOEL—JOHN DOMINIS—ALFRED EISENSTAEDT—DRAWING BY RENY MARTIN—NINA LEEN
15—COURTESY ART INSTITUTE OF CHICAGO, GIFT OF MR. & MRS. LEIGH B. BLOCK; JOHN LOENGARD—RALPH CRANE
16, 17—YALE JOEL
24, 25—FRANK SCHERSCHEL
28—HANK WALKER, FRANK SCHERSCHEL—FRANK SCHERSCHEL, HANK WALKER
28, 29—FRANK SCHERSCHEL (3), HANK WALKER (3)—FRANK SCHERSCHEL, HANK WALKER
30, 31—MARK KAUFFMAN
32, 33—LT. GEORGE SILK; GEN. GREY VILLET—GEORGE SILK, LT. GREY VILLET
34—CANADA PICTURES LTD.
35—FRANCIS MILLER, WALTER SANDERS—INT. JACK LINDSAY, WALTER SANDERS (2)
41—GORDON TENNEY FROM B.S.
42—GORDON TENNEY FROM B.S. EXC. BOT. RT. YALE JOEL
43—GORDON TENNEY FROM B.S.—YALE JOEL
49, 50—JAMES WHITMORE
52—JAMES WHITMORE EXC. BOT. U.P.
57—ALBERT FENN—TOM DEWBERRY
58—STAN WAYMAN FROM RAPHO-GUILLUMETTE
60—TOM DEWBERRY
62, 63—EXC. C. LT. A.P.
68—KEN MIDDLEHAM
74, 75—DRAWINGS BY RENY MARTIN
80—PARAMOUNT PICTURES—BILL AVERY FOR PARAMOUNT PICTURES
85—YALE JOEL
88—DRAWINGS BY GYO FUJIKAWA
89 THROUGH 92—NINA LEEN
93—PIERRE BOULAT, NINA LEEN
94, 95—NINA LEEN
96, 97—NINA LEEN
98—DAVID DOUGLAS DUNCAN—W.W.
100—NINA LEEN
105—HOWELL CONANT
109—GJON MILI
121—GEN. CHARLES PAYNE FROM N.Y. DAILY NEWS, BT. A.P.—CHARLES PAYNE FOR N.Y. DAILY NEWS
122—A.P. EXC. BOT. RT.
124—A.P., U.P.—CHICAGO SUN TIMES, U.P.
129—N.Y. JOURNAL-AMERICAN FROM INT.
130—JOHN DOMINIS
140—FROM "CHIANG KAI-SHEK" BY HOLLINGTON K. TONG, PUBLISHED BY THE CHINA PUBLISHING CO.; WU CHUNG YAT, A.P. U.P.
144—MAP BY H. E. SCOTT
150—A.P.
154—GEORGE RODGER
156—ALEXANDERON FROM RAPHO-GUILLUMETTE
161—FRANZ BERKO
162—FRANZ BERKO—MARGARET DURRANCE FROM RAPHO-GUILLUMETTE
164—LOUIS A. FRENCH

ABBREVIATIONS: BOT., BOTTOM; CEN., CENTER; EXC., EXCEPT; LT., LEFT; RT., RIGHT; T., TOP; A.P., ASSOCIATED PRESS; B.S., BLACK STAR; U.P., UNITED PRESS; W.W., WORLD; INT., INTERNATIONAL. THE ASSOCIATED PRESS IS EXCLUSIVELY ENTITLED TO REPUBLICATION WITHIN THE U.S. OF THE PICTURES HEREIN ORIGINATED OR DISTRIBUTED FROM THE ASSOCIATED PRESS.

LIFE, JUNE 24, 1957   VOLUME 42, NUMBER 25
LIFE IS PUBLISHED WEEKLY BY TIME INC., 540 N. MICHIGAN AVE., CHICAGO 11, ILL. PRINTED IN U.S.A. ENTERED AS SECOND-CLASS MATTER NOVEMBER 16, 1936 AT THE POST OFFICE AT CHICAGO, ILL. UNDER THE ACT OF MARCH 3, 1879, AUTHORIZED BY POST OFFICE DEPARTMENT, OTTAWA, CANADA, AS SECOND CLASS MATTER. SUBSCRIPTIONS $6.75 A YEAR IN U.S.A.; $7.75 IN CANADA.

EDITOR-IN-CHIEF............Henry R. Luce
PRESIDENT................Roy E. Larsen

MANAGING EDITOR
Edward K. Thompson
DEPUTY MANAGING EDITOR
Robert T. Elson
ASSISTANT MANAGING EDITORS
Philip H. Wootton Jr.
George P. Hunt

John K. Jessup..CHIEF EDITORIAL WRITER
Charles Tudor...................ART DIRECTOR
Joseph Kastner.................COPY EDITOR
Marian A. MacPhail..CHIEF OF RESEARCH
Ray Mackland.................PICTURE EDITOR

SENIOR EDITORS: Donald Bermingham, Gene Farmer, Jay Gold, William Gray, Kenneth MacLeish, Hugh Moffett, Tom Prideaux, Sam Welles.

STAFF WRITERS: Herbert Brean, William Brinkley, Roger Butterfield, Robert Coughlan, William Miller, John Osborne, Robert Wallace.

PHOTOGRAPHIC STAFF: Margaret Bourke-White, James Burke, Edward Clark, Ralph Crane, Loomis Dean, John Dominis, Alfred Eisenstaedt, Eliot Elisofon, J. R. Eyerman, N. R. Farbman, Andreas Feininger, Albert Fenn, Fritz Goro, Allan Grant, Yale Joel, Mark Kauffman, Robert W. Kelley, Dmitri Kessel, Nina Leen, Thomas McAvoy, Leonard McCombe, Francis Miller, Ralph Morse, Carl Mydans, Gordon Parks, Michael Rougier, Walter Sanders, Frank J. Scherschel, Joe Scherschel, Paul Schutzer, George Silk, Howard Sochurek, Peter Stackpole, Grey Villet, Hank Walker, James Whitmore.
ASSISTANT PICTURE EDITORS: Frank Campion, Lee Eitingon.
FILM EDITORS: Margaret Sargent, Nancy Bragdon, Barbara Brewster.

ASSOCIATE EDITORS: Oliver Allen, Ralph Graves, Mary Hamman, Jesse Hobing, Sally Kirkland, Marshall Smith, John Thorne, Keith Wheeler, A. B. C. Whipple, Warren Young.

ASSISTANT EDITORS: Robert Ajemian, David Bergamini, Earl Brown, Mathilde Camacho, Robert Campbell, Charles Champlin, Wilbur Cross, Anne Denny, John Dille, Robert Drew, Terry Drucker, Nancy Genet, William Goodrich Jr., Muriel Hall, Patricia Hunt, Edward Kern, Landon Haight, Jerry Korn, Mary Leatherbee, Jeanne LeMonnier, James Lipscomb, Richard Meryman Jr., Jack Newcombe, Eleanor Parish, Joseph Roddy, Albert Rosenfeld, Irene Saint, David Scherman, Dorothy Seiberling, Mary Lou Skinner, John Stanton, Valerie Vondermuhll, Loudon Wainwright.

REPORTERS: Virginia Addison, Michael J. Arlen, Linda Asher, Elizabeth Baker, Mary Elizabeth Barber, Margaret Bassett, Laura Bell, Patricia Blake, Peter Bunzel, Margery Byers, Vivian Campbell, Helen Carlton, Barbara Cummiskey, Laura Ecker, Barbara Ellis, Diana Fetter, Kim Freese, Joan Gibson, Frances Glennon, Lee Hall, Kathleen Hampton, Terry Harman, Judith Holden, Monica Horne, Alison Kallman, Nancy King, Richard Lewis, John MacDonald, Joann McQuiston, Jane Nelson, Loretta Nelson, Clara Nicolai, Sheila O'Connor, Charles Osborne, John Osmundsen, William Pain, Patsy Parkin, Patricia Phillips, Maya Pines, Norman Ritter, Ellyn Schiff, Kathleen Shortall, Ruth Silva, Jeanne Stahl, Helga Staudenberger, Marion Steinmann, Jean Strong, Marian Taylor, Lucy Thomas, Terry Turner, Don Underwood, Marilyn Wellemeyer, Thomas Wheeler, Margaret Williams, Jane Wilson, Alix Witteborg, Sharon Workman.

COPY READERS: Helen Deuell (Chief), Dorothy Ilson, Lu Burke, Barbara Fuller, Virginia Sadler, Marguerite Scheips, Suzanne Seixas, Rachel Tuckerman.

LAYOUT: Bernard Quint, David Stech (Associate Art Directors), Margit Varga, Robert Young (Assistant Art Directors), William Gallagher, Hilde Adelsberger, Matt Greene, Earle Kersh, Albert Ketchum, Anthony Sodaro, Richard Valdati, John Woods.

PICTURE BUREAU: Natalie Kosek (Chief), Mary Carr, Betty Doyle, Margaret Goldsmith, Ruth Lester, Maude Milar.

PHOTOGRAPHIC LABORATORY: William J. Sumits (Chief), George Karas.

PICTURE LIBRARY: Alma Eggleston (Chief), Doris O'Neil, Alberta Kreh.

U.S. & CANADIAN NEWS SERVICE: Lawrence Laybourne (Chief of Correspondents), Tom Carmichael, Helen Fennell, Marshall Lumsden, George McCue—WASHINGTON: James Shepley, Donald Wilson, Mary Cadwalader, Will Lang, Don Schanche, Hugh Sidey, Henry Suydam Jr.; CHICAGO: T. George Harris, Roy Rowan, Jane Estes, Leon Jaroff, John McDermott, William Trombley; LOS ANGELES: Frank McCulloch, John Jenkinson, Shana Alexander, James Goode, Frank Pierson, Davis Thomas, David Zeitlin; ATLANTA: Harry Fleischman; Robert Mason, Richard Stolley; BOSTON: William Johnson, Wilbur Jarvis; DALLAS: Willard Rappleye Jr., Jane Scholl; DENVER: Barron Beshoar, Bayard Hooper; DETROIT: Norman Nicholson, Richard Anthony; SAN FRANCISCO: Richard Pollard, John Porter; SEATTLE: Robert Schulman, Russell Sackett; OTTAWA: Arthur White, Ruth Mehrtens; MONTREAL: Byron Riggan; TORONTO: Murray Gart; CALGARY: Ed Ogle.

FOREIGN NEWS SERVICE: Manfred Gottfried (Chief of Correspondents), John Boyle; George Caturani—LONDON: Max Ways, Norman Ross, Beatrice Dobie, Harold Barden Morse; PARIS: Frank White, Milton Orshefsky, George Abell, Anne Chamberlin, Timothy Foote, Gabrielle Smith, David Snell; BONN: Edward Hughes, John Mulliken; ROME: Walter Guzzardi, Don Jane Hamblin; ATHENS: Donald Burke; ISTANBUL: Robert Neville; BEIRUT: John Mecklin; NEW DELHI: James L. Greenfield; HONG KONG: James Bell, Jack Lerner; TOKYO: Curtis Prendergast, Alexander Campbell; MEXICO CITY: Richard Oulahan Jr.; GUATEMALA CITY: Harvey Rosenhouse; RIO DE JANEIRO: Piero Saporiti; BUENOS AIRES: Philip Payne.

PUBLISHER............Andrew Heiskell
ADVERTISING DIRECTOR....Clay Buckhout

A Farewel

In black-gowned ranks the Class of '57, 300,000 strong, assemble
campuses across the country for the rituals of graduation. The occa
marked the completion of academic work and a step into another w
But, as it always has, it marked much more than this to the depa
seniors. To 21-year-old Roger Dennis Hansen (*left*) and his 933 u
mates at Yale, it meant the bittersweet end to four fruitful under
uate years. Hansen had already prepared himself during the pre
days of graduation week for this moment by severing, as gently a
could, some of the ties which bound him to his alma mater.

For the most part, the last week at Yale was a time for fun ra
than for nostalgia. Hansen had had a fine life at Yale. He had mad

TRYING ON COSTUME three days before graduation, Yale Senior Roger
Hansen claps on a mortarboard. He paid $3.25 for the rented cap and gown. He
wore them three times—at baccalaureate (*right*), class day and commencement.

"HOLY, HOLY, HOLY" rises to the vaulted roof of Woolsey Hall, where
seniors massed in the center, with families and guests around them and crowd-
ing the galleries, sing the hymn during the religious service of baccalaureate.

Photographed for LIFE by ALFRED EISENSTAEDT

o Bright College Years

Kappa, been on the swimming team, won a Rhodes scholarship to rd, been elected to Scroll and Key, one of the college's exclusive t societies. Now, taking his final fling at the life he had enjoyed so a, Hansen forgot about sleep and plunged into an exhausting round lebrations. But between partying and listening misty-eyed to the Vienpoofs, Hansen found time to make lingering farewell visits to his a and favorite professors, whom he might never meet again. hen at the end of the week his parents arrived from California, en proudly showed them around his campus. At a party in his s, which he had only just finished cleaning, Hansen introduced to some of the people who had been so much of his life at Yale.

The climax of commencement drew on. Capped and gowned, Hansen took his place amid his classmates for baccalaureate service (*below*) and the president's address. Then came the festivities of class day, the awarding of honors, the reading of the class poem, the singing of the old Yale song, *Bright College Years*. Next morning an audience of thousands assembled on the sun-dappled lawns of the Old Campus for the commencement ceremony. Hansen, as a class marshal, picked up a pack of diplomas for his own Silliman College, one of 10 undergraduate houses. Later, in the intimate surroundings of Silliman quadrangle, he stepped up once more for his diploma and this time, for Roger Dennis Hansen B.A. Universitatis Yalensis, the bright years slid irrevocably into the past.

CONTINUED

Packing, proud parents, and a prom

PLEASANT ENCOUNTER took place after baccalaureate when Hansen met Mrs. Juan Trippe, wife of PanAm's chairman. Her son is also Yale '57.

FATHER MEETS ROOMMATE at the party the boys gave for their parents, as Hansen makes introduction to Ian Henderson (*left*). This was the fir...

AT AN INFORMAL PARTY IN HIS ROOMS BEFORE THE SENIOR PROM, HANSEN PLAYFULLY TRIES TO SNATC...

HOUSECLEANING their rooms, Hansen and his roommates, William Thieme (*left*) and Joe Clayton (*center*), go over rug with borrowed vacuum cleaner.

PACKING BOOKS, Hansen lifts an armful, mostly volumes on history, his major. Some he sent home to San Carlos, Calif. Others he sold to students.

either of his parents had ever seen Yale. Clar- Hansen, an ex-sea captain, works as inspector a marine insurance company in San Francisco.

MOTHER MEETS MOTHER as Henderson and Hansen look on. Mrs. Hansen (*left*) gets to know Mrs. Gerald Neary, mother of another roommate.

PRESIDENTIAL GREETING is bestowed on Hansen at reception after baccalaureate by Dr. A. Whitney Griswold. He knew Hansen for good record.

PHONE AWAY FROM DATE, SUE KIRK, A SMITH COLLEGE SOPHOMORE

AT THE PROM, Hansen guides Sue across the floor of New Haven Lawn Club. Later they all sat around on the floor to hear the Whiffenpoofs sing. Hansen did not get to bed until 5 but was up next morning in time to see Sue off at 9:30,

CONTINUED 133

89

Commencement's solemn ritu

LEADING THE SENIORS to class day ceremonies, Hansen carries banner as, preceded by campus policeman, he passes through gates to Old Campus.

COMMENCEMENT, Yale's 256th, is held on shaded Old Campus. There were 7,000 guests. Hansen received diplomas for Silliman classm

IN THOUGHTFUL MOMENT Hansen (*second from left*) stands with Roommate Joseph Clayton (*left*) and two classmates (*right*), waiting for commencement procession to form. Clayton is head of glee club and member of Whiffenpoofs.

GETTING HIS DIPLOMA in Silliman College quadrangle, Hansen tak from Dr. Luther Noss, master of Silliman. When Hansen read diploma late learned for first time that he had graduated *magna cum laude*—with high hor

and a diploma

NOSTALGIC CHORUS during glee club concert brings audience to its feet, waving handkerchiefs and singing, "For God, for country, and for Yale!"

FAREWELL TO A FRIEND brings Hansen to Yale's great swimming coach, Bob Kiphuth. Kiphuth became fond of Hansen, who was a short-distance star. Here Kiphuth explains to Hansen, who will teach swimming at camp this summer, how to use bamboo pole to prod swimmers to the side of a pool for instruction. With this, Hansen said goodby to the man who, he says, had done more for him at Yale than anyone else, and then left the pool where he had won his cherished Y.

136

Tanning Pix

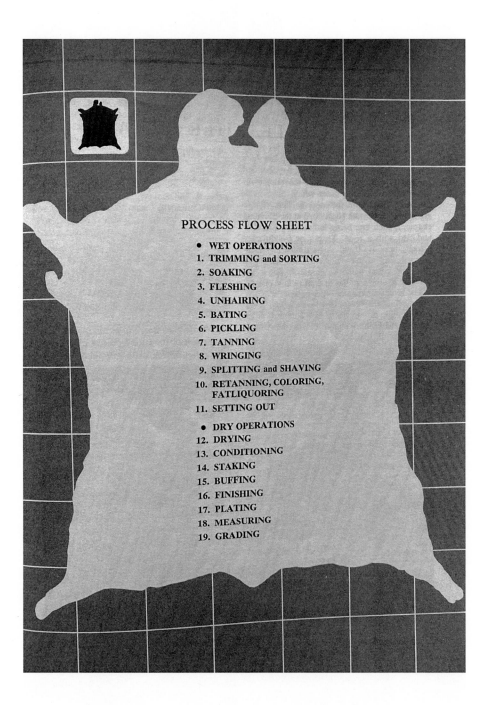

PROCESS FLOW SHEET

- **WET OPERATIONS**
1. **TRIMMING and SORTING**
2. **SOAKING**
3. **FLESHING**
4. **UNHAIRING**
5. **BATING**
6. **PICKLING**
7. **TANNING**
8. **WRINGING**
9. **SPLITTING and SHAVING**
10. **RETANNING, COLORING, FATLIQUORING**
11. **SETTING OUT**

- **DRY OPERATIONS**
12. **DRYING**
13. **CONDITIONING**
14. **STAKING**
15. **BUFFING**
16. **FINISHING**
17. **PLATING**
18. **MEASURING**
19. **GRADING**

[LEFT] Siding hides; Hides are "green salted" or brine cured in a raceway and then bundled singly before they are loaded onto a truck for shipment to a tannery. They are heavy, many weighing over 75 lbs, and to make them easier to process they are usually cut into sides.

[RIGHT] Loading sides into paddle vats; Half round vats, equipped with paddle wheels like those on an old river steamboat are used to keep sides moving in the tanning "liquors" with which they are filled. These paddles rotate throughout two stages of the tanning process, soaking and unhairing, in which the sides are immersed in these vats, In between these two baths, the sides are "fleshed". This is done on a large machine with two cylinders, one ridged and one bladed that is rotating in the opposite direction and cuts away flesh remaining on the side after slaughter. [CAPTION FOR NEXT PHOTO BOTTOM OF FACING PAGE]

Loading sides into rotating drums of various types and sizes are used in a number of processes in the tanning of leather, in bating, pickling, tanning, coloring, fatliquoring and dry milling. There have been many changes in drum design, in the materials from which they are made and in the control systems used to insure uniformity from batch to batch, of the leather being processed in them.

Ellithorp Tannery circa 1952. Thee tannery no longer exists. Closed in 1987 and razed not long thereafter, the property remains a fenced in "brown field".

Scudding sides; In unhairing, the hair on a side is dissolved, its epidermis is loosened, and certain soluble skin proteins are removed. Depending on the strength of the unhairing bath, there may still be some dissolved hair left in the hair follicles. When 'Dave and I worked at W&JM this was removed by scudding. Today, this job is done on an unhairing machine, identical in operation to a fleshing machine but with a blunt, rather than bladed cylinder doing the necessary squeezing.

THINGS

A Few of My Favorite Things

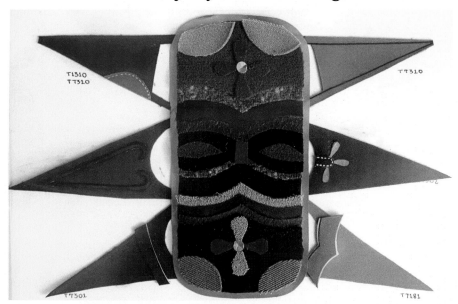

A Leather Collection presentation designed to tell the story of the colors and textures of the leathers shown to prospective customers in the showroom of Hermann Loewenstein Inc.

H. & M Rayne, Ltd., of England, have been the court shoemakers by appointment of the King for many years. For the coronation of King George VI, pink suede shoes were ordered for the two young princesses, Elizabeth and Margaret Rose. Since only the finest leather can go into the shoes of the royal family, especially for such an occasion, Hermann Loewenstein was given the honor of manufacturing the pink suede for these shoes. You are now looking at the same leather that was in the shoes worn by Elizabeth Regina II, the present Queen, on the historic occasion of her father's coronation in 1937.

H&M Rayne made shoes out of Loewenstein leathers for Queen Elizabeth. The leather in this photo is a pink suede that Rayne used when he crafted Princess Margaret's wedding shoes.

REFER TO _____

ARMY SERVICE FORCES
Office of the Quartermaster General
WASHINGTON 25, D. C.

19 December 1945

Mr. Rudolph Correll, President
Leach-Heckel Leather Company
Salem, Massachusetts.

Dear Mr. Correll:

This office wishes to express its appreciation and commendation to you and the personnel of your company for the loyalty, unceasing effort, and many contributions afforded the Quartermaster Corps during the past few years.

Your excellent work and technical assistance in connection with the development and production of Mukluk leather are fully recognized and greatly appreciated by the entire Quartermaster Corps. No one realizes more than this office the importance of the time, effort, and skill which have been so fully devoted by your company in helping this office to improve the above item for use by troops in the field.

I personally want you to know that your many contributions will long be remembered and recognized by the Quartermaster Corps as playing a vital part in the total effort to help bring victory to our Country. It is hoped that you will continue to be interested in our post-war program of improving existing Quartermaster items and in the development of new ones.

Very truly yours,

GEORGES F. DORIOT
Brigadier General, QMC
Director, Military Planning Division

A letter of commendation to Dad, thanking him for the work he did developing a leather for mukluks. These boots, used by the U.S. Army in World War II when fighting in freezing conditions, proved highly effective in preventing frostbite.

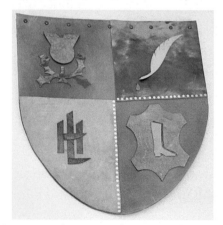

Bill Martin presented me with this shield in 1983 when I gave up my post as president of Hermann Loewenstein and enrolled in the Yale School of Organization and Management. Its symbols tell stories and ring bells for me.

Tomahawk, my dad's picture-perfect white, Alden design yawl, a photo taken by Stanley Rosenfield, a well-known marine photographer

A signet ring bearing the Correll family crest. The genealogical research that followed the Correll family line back to an ancestor who made firearms for the Duke of Alba in Spain was done by Dad's sister Elizabeth, who decided to build the family tree of her mother, Helene Correll, rather than her father's Loewenstein family lineage.

A wall of memories in my office at home in Johnstown.

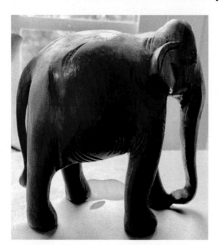

A wooden elephant, acquired by Mom's stepfather, Dr. Karl Geronne, while serving in South Africa during the Boer War as a doctor in the German army.

ACT 3: AT FINISHING SCHOOL

SCENE 1:

The Shortest, Gladdest Years of Life
1953-1957, 1984-1985

Learning how to be a leatherman was not all the learning I wanted to do. I needed to broaden my horizons, to learn how to learn. Dad had not gone to college. He had gone right into the business after he graduated from prep school. I went to Yale, two times around, as an undergraduate in 1953 and, in 1984 as a student at its School of Management. When I first walked through the doors of Hermann Loewenstein after graduation in 1957, a full-time employee now, Dad took me aside. "Son, you can forget everything you learned at Yale now," he told me. "You're in the real world." For years I found this advice denigrating. Okay, Dad, I thought. Then why did you send me to Yale? Do you think what I learned there won't help me be a better leatherman?

I've often wondered what caused him to choose those words to welcome me. I had gone to Lawrenceville, the school he attended and wanted me to go to. I had played football there like he had. I was recruited by Yale's coach, Jordan Oliver, to come to Yale, not Princeton which was the default choice for Lawrentians. I had graduated from Lawrenceville with honors and from Yale with a gentleman's B. I had agonized, which he must have sensed, over the decision to come work for him. I had gotten good job offers from two Fortune 500 companies. I was, and still am, I guess, a person who needs praise. I am energized by it and despondent without it. When that praise wasn't forthcoming, when it seemed that he was denigrating what I had learned, I felt despondent, a feeling that returned, for many years every time the memory of that initial greeting came to mind.

I see things differently now. When I went back to Yale, to the School of Management, I resonated with what I was learning. The words coming out of our professors' mouths opened my ears to new ideas and ways

of looking at problems. Much of what they said, the theories they es-
poused, the hypotheses they drew made sense and answered questions I'd
struggled with as a leatherman. But some didn't and at age 50, with 35
years of business experience, I wasn't shy anymore, spoke up and brought
some real-world experience into the classroom. One interaction, a cameo,
is one of my favorite memories of my days at SOM. Richard Hackman,
a professor for whom I had utmost respect, was dissecting a case study
on leadership styles. The class was a small one and Richard was waxing
poetic about his favorite topic, self-managing groups. His approach made
real sense and caused me to share an experience I'd encountered during
my years in the leather business. He weighed my words, smiled broadly
and posed a facetious question to me and the group. "Correll, are you the
student here or the teacher?" It was exhilarating to hear those words of
approbation, an acceptance of the importance real world situations and
solutions. As I write these lines, it also makes me realize the gifts my father gave me, as he prepared me for his real world, creating opportunities
to learn and then letting me find my own way through them.

The learning I did at Yale as an undergraduate was less than it could
or should have been. I was smart enough to compete, eager enough to
learn but too shy to speak up in class or take advantage of the opportunities to interact with my teachers. I kept on the straight and narrow pretty
much and kept my head down most of the time. But I wasn't a recluse. I
could be seen, with buddies from the football team, at one of the tables
down at Mory's, drinking its famous green cups and singing Yale songs,
including its alma mater, "Bright College Years." I've sung this melody
countless times since I graduated from Yale. Its nostalgic lyrics bring back
many memories, some happy, some sad, some wistful. And on reflection,
I did learn something that proved critical in my career as a leatherman. I
learned how to learn, to decide, to verbalize, to act and interact.

My undergraduate years at Yale started off well. After four years away
as a prep school boarder at Lawrenceville, the transition to college life in
New Haven was relatively seamless. The professors teaching the electives
I chose, philosophy, political science and history of art and architecture,
were charismatic, Yale's very best. The course materials were stimulating,
provoking thoughts and a dream, a very faint one that caused me to wonder. Could I become a professor?

Life on the football field was exciting as well. Butting heads with an array of all-state players during a training exercise called Bull in the Ring was a new, sobering experience that caused me to wonder. Do I have it in me to compete against that kind of talent? I remember driving home after a Friday practice, thinking that maybe I should quit. That thought vanished, however, after I switched on the TV and watched a college football game that Saturday and saw how those guys, a Division 1 team, were blocking. I can do that as well, maybe even better than those guys, I reasoned. That decided, I returned to New Haven the next day, ready to put on the pads for Monday's freshman football team practice session. In those days, Yale fielded a freshman team. The Bullpups, they were called, and in 1953, when I played on that team, we were damn good, undefeated as a matter of fact. Just being a member of that team and playing for Gib Holgate, our inspirational, innovative coach, was a high point of my four years as an undergraduate. Gib had a way of bringing out the best in all of his players. He sure did with me. I never played as well, before or after. And then, when Wayne Moeller got injured and I won the starting position at left tackle, boy, that was a heady experience.

Things were also going well in my freshman dorm on the old campus. Peter Cooke and Jay Inglis, my roommates in our third-floor, three-man suite in Welsh Hall, were nice guys and we were hitting it off nicely. I was making other friends on the football team and in my classes, friendships, some of which have lasted a lifetime. Last but not least was the social scene. By the time I went off to Yale and Chloe to Goucher, she and I were almost an item. With close to 300 miles separating us, and little likelihood of seeing each other frequently, we were dating other people. But where there's a will, there's a way and, that fall she came up to New Haven from Baltimore by train for a football weekend. A Goucher-approved residence was found for her to stay in, a stipulation issued in those days, for her protection. We made the most of her stay, enjoying each other's company as we went out for dinner, to a glee club concert at Woolsey Hall and walked, hand in hand, around the Yale campus. That might not be enough action for today's collegians but it sufficed for us, for the time being.

Later that year, I drove down to Towson with Bill Farley, a freshman football teammate and roommate-to-be, for dates with Chloe and a friend of hers at Goucher. That trip was especially memorable because of the free housing Bill was able to arrange for us. Thanks to his dad, a policeman in Salt Lake City, we were welcome to stay at the police station in Towson, near the college. Our bedroom was a bit larger than most, a lighted courtroom where we slept on two wooden benches. After six hours on the road, those benches, hard as they were, did not keep us from sleeping.

Keeping our long-distance romance alive with trips like these and dates at home during vacations, we were growing closer but still not quite ready to commit to going steady. With Annapolis nearby, Goucher girls were often invited to dances at the Naval Academy. Chloe attended several and was dating a midshipman for a brief period of time. As for me, friends were arranging dates at Smith and other nearby women's colleges. My trusty blue VW bug was constantly on the move, putting on quite a few miles. Life was good, rife with pleasures, at least for now.

Sophomore year started off with a bang. I was switched from tackle to guard on the 1955 varsity team and started in Yale's first game that season, a tilt with the University of Connecticut. A picture of me blocking for our fullback, appeared in the New Haven Register that Sunday, with the caption, "Correll guides Corelli", a copy of which found its way into the shop window of Fenn-Feinstein, a men's haberdashery located on Broadway near the Yale Co-op. I basked in this moment of celebrity. Fraternity rushing came shortly thereafter. DKE was after many of my football teammates and I felt a bit let down that they were not chasing me. But Phi Gam was a more than acceptable alternative, a place where I felt at home and made good friends. Academically, things were in order. I was firmly on track towards my declared major, chemical engineering. Things looked promising. Then all of a sudden, I started the nosedive that marked the rest or my undergraduate experience at Yale.

The same thing began to happen on the football field. Today there are teams that take the field for offense, defense, kickoffs, etc. In those days we were expected to play both ways. I was good on offense, quick off the mark and blocked well. That's why I got that shot at playing guard when we moved up to the varsity. Defense was another matter. I was shorter, lighter and not savvy enough about what I could expect when the ball was snapped. I had a lot to learn and hoped coach Oliver and his assistants would spend more time working with less than superstar players like me. He didn't. He was a good recruiter. He fielded Ivy League championship teams and compiled a 96-34 record during the nine years he coached the Elis. But he was not an inspirational coach. I needed attention and praise to be a really good player. I didn't get it, my hopes of being a regular started fading away. Oliver was not a Holgate or a Tiihonen, my coach at Lawrenceville. From there on out, after that UConn game, football lost much of its allure. I stayed on the squad, though and played first string in all the JV games during my sophomore and junior years. I would have continued playing football as a senior had it not been for a neck injury suffered during a preseason workout. It's easy to imagine the pleasure I had being a member of the championship team that upset Army 14-12 in 1955. It's tougher perhaps to imagine the disappointment I've felt that I never got my Major Y. Because of that damn injury I was sitting in the stands instead of on the bench as Yale beat Harvard, quite handily, during my senior year. Had I been, that letter would have been mine, as Oliver emptied the bench to give all hands that prize.

In the classroom, things were also starting to go downhill. Chemistry, a course I had aced at Lawrenceville, was giving me problems. As we got into organic chemistry the As that had been so easy to get at prep school were turning into Cs.. Calculus was also giving me fits. I blamed that on the teacher, a Mr. Peepers. I was so good at math at Lawrenceville, why not here at Yale? This shouldn't be happening. But it was and it looked like there might be some dark days ahead. That being the case, the dean of the Engineering School called me in for a chat. After asking some pertinent questions about my performance, my career goals and hearing me out, he suggested I consider switching my major to IA, industrial administration, Yale's business major. I knew my dad would be disappointed. He wanted me to be a leatherman and that, to him, meant that I must know my chemistry. Ergo, major in chemical engineering. But what the dean was saying seemed reasonable. An IA major, aimed at making me a good businessman, would serve me far better than continuing my pursuit of a degree in chemical engineering, offering courses that were not aimed at producing hotshot tanners. I suspected Dad would not be happy that I dropped out. "Corrells stay the course," he used to say. "They never quit!" But the dean's explanation was enough for me. I readily accepted his suggestion to switch my major to IA. As things turned out, that was a good decision.

So was my decision on residential colleges and roommates in my sophomore year. I opted for a spacious quad on the third floor of a corner entryway in South Berkeley. I knew two of my roommates already. Bill Farley and Richard Hanks had been teammates of mine on the Bullpups. Our fourth in our quad was Tim Childs. None of us knew Tim before then, but he turned out to be a good egg. The four of us, however, were as different as fish and fowl. Richard and Bill were Mormons, straight arrows, strait-laced and by then, married, unbeknownst to Yale, and living off campus. Tim was unique, a bon vivant who came from a family that had the money to afford the very best. Among the belongings he brought with him was a top-of-the-line HMV record player and an extensive library of records. Tim loved classical music and it permeated the common room of our quad whenever he was not in class. I can see him now, sitting in an overstuffed leather armchair, engrossed in a book, a glass of single malt Scotch or bourbon in one of his hands. Tim was an eccentric in a charming way.

There is a story about the birthday party Tim hosted for himself in our quad common room that is too delicious to ignore. After one round of drinks, he suggested we play a game that required a degree of dexterity and sobriety. Wooden sticks, equal in length, standing on their ends were fashioned into a teepee-like structure in the middle of our room. Each guest, in turn, was asked to remove one of these sticks without causing the teepee to collapse. If the removal of a player's stick was successful, the communal shot glass, filled with the best Scotch money could buy, was passed on to the next man to his left. If the teepee collapsed, however, a penalty was assessed. The contents of the shot glass had to be downed by the teepee destroyer, in a single gulp. The results are not hard to imagine and as contestants inevitably fell prey to the spirits they'd drunk, they dropped out, literally. Luckily Richard and Bill, who were standing in the shadows, picked up the pieces, escorting guests back to their rooms and tucking Tim and me into bed as well. A lesson was learned. It was not on the Yale curriculum, but the lesson I learned that night about the dangers of drinking too much hard liquor was a valuable one. It certainly had no bearing on my becoming a leatherman, but I must say I am struck by this parallel; the liquor we imbibe and the fat liquor used to make leather soft should both be carefully chosen and measured.

Our quad quartet split up at the end of our sophomore year. Bill left Yale shortly thereafter and Richard, while still listed as a resident of Berkeley, made his off-campus housing status official. Tim who had preferred a single in the first place, got his wish. I moved into another quad with another Rod (Rodney Farrow), Bill Olsen and Dave Lawrence. We were a compatible foursome. I liked rooming with all of them. There seemed no good reason not to continue to do so, but when it came time to decide on senior housing, I opted for a single.

A time clock started ticking early even before I made that choice about moving into a single. It began counting down at the start of my junior year and got louder as the year progressed. In less than two years I would have to decide to go or not to go work for my dad. This decision spooked me. I was not ready to do so yet, but the time was fast approaching to when I had no choice but to make one. This had two components, the first one strategic, objective, based on data. The other was interpersonal, subjective, based on feelings.

Strategically, our company, so successful and profitable during Dad's reign, looked like it might encounter some serious problems in the not-too-distant future. High-grade women's shoes from Italy, brands, like Magli and Ferragamo, could now be seen in upscale shoe salons all over the country. This footwear was highly styled, better quality and less expensive. Stores like Saks, Neiman Marcus, I. Magnin, to name a few, were starting to feature these shoes in their salons and they were flying off the shelves. This spelled trouble for our customers and, if this swing to imports grew, factories would start to close and our sales would suffer.

Another challenge strategically was the decreasing supply and increasing price of calfskin, our primary raw material. In Italy, vitello, veal, was the meat of preference. That ensured a steady supply of calfskins for Italian tanners at more or less stable prices. This was not the case here. In the U.S., the taste for red meat, beef, was growing, causing a decrease in the slaughter of calves and an increase in the prices paid for their skins. Leather made out of calfskins had been a high-grade shoemaker's leather of choice, but this was changing. As our raw material costs increased, so did the prices of our calfskin leathers. Needing to compete with cheaper imports, our customers were starting to switch to kidskin. In the old days, when my grandfather ran the firm, we sold a lot of kidskin leather, in one color, black. In 1956, kid-

skin, in all the colors of the rainbow, could be bought from Shrut & Asch, a firm run by George Shrut, a man in temperament, tactics and taste, quite similar to Dad. His firm was doing well but, with these two strikes against us I wondered, could Loewenstein prosper when Dad died and I took over?

Last but not least was the threat that products like DuPont's Corfam might someday put tanneries the world over out of business. Prior to its development, no synthetic fabric claimed to be as breathable as leather, an important feature when it came to assuring comfort to someone wearing a pair of shoes made out of it. With its reputation for technological innovation, its marketing prowess, its deep pockets and seemingly impressive data to back up its claim, the threat DuPont imposed, was considerable.

There were interpersonal reasons as well that caused me to struggle with my decision where to work. The first was maintaining my self-respect. Since when I was a kid, Dad had orchestrated what I did, and I went along with his plans throughout my youth. I was happy the way things had worked out. No complaints, no worries. I met and worked with a lot of interesting people. I traveled to fascinating places. The variables involved in making and selling leather intrigued rather than scared me. I really loved leather. It was in my blood, but I did not love Dad pushing me into a career. This decision I wanted to be my own. And, as a sidebar, I wanted to make sure, if I decided to go work for him, that he was not the only one making me a job offer.

Another reason, really a phobia, was my fear of feedback. As his first-born son, it was expected that I would ultimately become boss. That's the way primogeniture works, doesn't it? That was my assumption and, I have no doubt at all, that all of Dad's employees at Loewenstein expected this to be the case. As such, even as a kid, I was treated with the greatest respect. Somewhere along the line, however, I wondered what people were saying behind my back. I also started questioning their sincerity when they complimented my performance. But I did not question them about how they felt or insist on candid feedback. Worse yet, I did not give them candid feedback on their performance. I let things ride in order to avoid making waves and getting caught in any undertow. Wondering what people are thinking, saying and hiding can be dealt with. But I had not yet learned how to do this and wasn't sure I ever could, working for my dad at Hermann Loewenstein.

And finally, as I pondered whether to come work for him, another vexing thought kept coming up. It had nothing to do with Dad's forceful nature or the future of the business. It was the name of the business, our family's business. It was the shadow of my Jewish heritage, born a Loewenstein, masquerading as a Correll. That, I suspected, might have been the reason one of the spooks had not knocked on my door on Tap Day at Yale. It was a fear I harbored; that the thin veil of secrecy created by our name change would be forever pierced if I decided to work for Hermann Loewenstein after I graduated. I had been brought up a Christian. Our name was Jewish but I knew nothing about Judaism or about my ancestors' devotion to it or lack thereof. I felt caught in a trap not of my own making. I was confused, unsure of which way to turn. I was angry, feeling forced to make a decision. I was depressed, feeling that I was not fitting in and fearing that this situation would only get worse if I went to work at Hermann Loewenstein. And so I turned inward during my senior year at Yale and never returned for reunions of the Class of '57 until after I returned to Yale as a member of the SOM Class of '85. That experience was altogether different. I felt accepted, lock, stock and barrel.

The first evidence of my malaise as a Yale undergraduate was the mononucleosis I contracted halfway through the football season during my junior year. I remember vividly the JV game I played in at West Point. The lethargy, the screwups, the depression which ensued afterwards, led to all sorts of psychological testing. I was being taught how to make good business decisions in my IA courses. I was learning how to measure risks and rewards, to list pros and cons. And yet I could not face making this decision. I was hiding from, not confronting it. This had to stop!

Push finally came to shove one lovely, cloudless summer day in 1956. As dad and I were crossing the Triborough Bridge, headed for our office on Ferry St. in his turquoise Thunderbird convertible, he turned to me briefly and popped the question. "Have you decided what you want to do after you graduate." He wanted to know *now*. It was in midsummer, just before I would be returning to Yale for my senior year. The summer had been set aside for meeting customers in New York City and, later on, in New England. Today I would be visiting the offices of two of our best customers, Herbert Levine and David Evans, with our sales manager, Charles Recht. Charlie had taken me under his wing.

I liked him and was looking forward to my day, but Dad's question stopped me dead in my tracks.

I had given it a lot of thought. Despite all my reservations, I was inclined to say yes, I will come to work for you. But I was not ready yet to tell him that. I did not want to be locked in, and as we drove onto the East River Drive and headed downtown, I gave him an answer. Giving life to the dream I once had in freshman year, I told him, "I think I'd like to be a teacher, a professor, just like Grandpere once hoped he could be." It did not take Dad more than a few seconds to reply, "Son, teachers are wimps. Listen to me, please. You will be better off in the leather business." And that was the end of our discussion. But it was not the end of my inner turmoil, not until I decided to interview with two major Fortune 500 companies, Dupont and Proctor & Gamble. And, guess what, I got good job offers from both of them. That was all I needed to make my decision. I decided to roll the dice and come work for Dad.

SCENE 2:

Forming Relationships with Customers and Suppliers

1953-1956

A Tour of European Tanneries – 1953

The year after Dave and I spent our summer across the pond, Dad planned another trip to Europe for me. I had just graduated from Lawrenceville that June and this trip was billed as a graduation present, the "grand tour" that was offered to eligible offspring at times like these in days of yore. In this case, however, there would be no chaperones, only my Lawrenceville roommates, Clarence "Ren" Zimmerman and Pete Balbach. Their fathers were not the traveler that Dad was, so they left all the details up to him. He took on the responsibility with relish. This time there would be no freighters, no youth hostels or bikes involved. We were armed with wallets of American Express traveler's checks, not enough currency to live high off the hog but plenty to complete the circuit Dad laid out for us. That itinerary, which had Dad's fingerprints all over it, took us through countryside, to small towns and into cities. The experiences would be memorable, for all of us, and many would allow us to spin some rather delicious tales for family and friends in the future We were, in a sense, as free as larks. But there was a subtext; we would visit all the tanneries in the U.K. and Europe that supplied leather to Hermann Loewenstein. Ren and Pete agreed that was not too much to ask. For me, it paid one other dividend; it would provide introductions to men and women, who would have a direct impact on me in the future. The plan laid out for us was as follows.

Our trip would begin in New York, at Idlewild Airport. We would fly to London aboard a Pan Am Stratocruiser, a flight that took just over 18 hours with stops in Gander, Newfoundland, and Shannon, Ireland. Flying cut down dramatically on the 12 days Dave and I had spent getting over to the U.K. by sea. That gave us more time to tour and sightsee. Our itinerary was equally appealing. We would meet Mom and Dad and check in at their hotel in London. The Ritz was way above our pay grade, but with dad paying the bill for the high tea we had there that afternoon and the roast beef dinner they treated us to at Simpson's in the Strand, we were still solvent when we left the next day and headed north. Our means of conveyance was a white Hillman Minx Dad had bought to do a tour of the U.K. and the continent. "Peter Rabbit," as they had christened it, would take us first to Troon where we would spend the night with the Martins at Dunchattan. From there dad's plan was for us to drive south and east to Harwich where we would catch a ferry to the Hook of Holland. And then, our tour of Europe would start, full swing.

In total, we went through or touched down in 10 countries, the Netherlands, Belgium, Luxembourg, France, Italy, Monaco, West Germany, Austria, Switzerland and Liechtenstein. The route Dad had devised could not have been more enticing. We spent time in a number of major cities, Amsterdam, the Hague, Paris, Rome and Milan, some sizable ones like Strasburg, Salzburg and Heidelberg, and at some tourist destinations such as the Black Forest, the Matterhorn and the French and Italian Rivieras. Patched in between these ports of call were the anchors of Dad's plan for us, visits to the tanneries Loewenstein did business with, or used to do business with. These included tanneries in France, Les Tanneries du Puy in Le Puy, Tanneries Cara in Romans and Tanneries Haas in Barr. In Germany we visited, the Carl Freudenberg tannery in Weinheim and J. Mayer & Sohn in Offenbach am Main. And in Italy, in Torino, we met the owner, toured his tannery and had a chance to see and touch the exquisite heavyweight, shrunken grain leather it made out of bovine shoulders.

Laying out a grand tour like this one, combining business with pleasure, making sure there were plenty of highlights, was one of Dad's specialties. Without question, top billing on this one was our three-day stay in Paris. Jean Compard, brother of the artist Emile Compard, was Loewenstein's agent at the time. He lived in Paris and was asked to book us rooms in an inexpensive small hotel on the Left Bank. Our rooms were small, on the third floor with no elevator to take us up or down. But they were clean, the beds were comfortable and "Madame" was pleasant, willing to provide us with advice on what to see, where to eat and get things we needed. So was Jean, who took us under his wing and saw to it that we got a real taste of Paris. That included things like having café au lait and croissants at breakfast, biting into a croque monsieur and downing a French biere somewhere, sampling belon oysters at La Coupole, checking out the scene at Deux Magots and enjoying the passing parade as we sat at an outside table at one of the cafes on the Champs Elysée. Ren and I were ready for all of this and we soaked it up voraciously. Pete was more conservative, a meat and potatoes guy who was always looking for where he could get a Coke, a hamburger and American, not French style, French fries. He perked up a bit when we went to Montmartre to check out the Folies Bergère and other action in that Quarter. He was also eager to see the Eiffel Tower and keen to drive Peter Rabbit around the rotary that encircles the Arc du Triomphe. This visit was just a foretaste, but that was enough to make us all happy and want to return. Trips to Paris in later years opened my eyes to many of the other special things Paris has to offer. I love London but there's nothing quite like Paris.

Two other special moments occurred which involved members of my family. The first was a meeting with Sturla Gudlaugson, the son of my Omi's sister. The second was short visit with my mother's sister-in-law, Rosa Wessel. Uncle Sturla, an art historian whose research focused on the painter Gerard ter Borch, was the head of the Mauritshuis museum in the Hague. Besides being highly respected for his seminal work on this Dutch Golden Age artist, Sturla, was a really nice guy. He greeted us warmly, gave us a guided tour of his museum and then took us out to an Indonesian restaurant for a rijsttafel lunch. Museum tours were not something I was used to. Neither was a meal as varied and delicious as Indonesian rijsttafel. Both were enjoyable.

In Liechtenstein, in Schaan, we met up with Rosa and her husband, Ernst Wessel, Mom's older brother, and had another lovely visit. The Correll kids knew their Uncle Ernst and Tante Rosl well, but only from, afar. Each Christmas and on our birthdays, we got Swiss chocolates from Tante Rosl, a treat we all thoroughly enjoyed. We'd heard many stories about my aunt and uncle from Omi and Mom but I had never met either of them until then. I knew that they had emigrated from Germany shortly before World War II broke out and that Rosl, had worked closely with the inventor of the cough medicine Pertussin. I'd heard that she had been deputized to build and run a factory to manufacture this medication in Vaduz, Liechtenstein's capital city. I suspected that she was a rather exceptional woman to be able to carry this off but had not the slightest conception about what it must have taken to turn this venture into a success. Uncle Ernst was a lovely, gentle man. who, because of a heart condition, stayed pretty much in the background. It was Rosl who ruled the Wessel roost, a tiger, someone I got to know well, respect and love in the years that followed. Mom accepted her. She was her beloved brother's wife. But she did not seem to love her. Why she felt that way is a mystery, one that I ponder as I write these lines. Perhaps it was Rosl's strength and willingness to fight for what she wanted?

Other family, or soon to be family affairs, cropped up during the course of our trip. The first, a small world experience, happened on the Italian Riviera. We had heard a lot about the small town of Portofino. We wanted to see it but, being on a limited budget, decided to stay overnight in an el cheapo hotel in nearby Santa Margherita. The following day, we piled into Peter Rabbit, headed east to Portofino, parked the car and started walking along the waterfront. It's an artist's delight, colorful, picturesque, captivating. I sort of expected to be struck by the beauty of the colorful buildings lining its harbor but I did not expect to bump into family. But lo and behold, I did. There on the waterfront, walking towards us, was my father's not-so-favorite nephew, my cousin Peter Lewis. Belying his reputation, Peter was very gracious. He invited us to lunch at one of Portofino's waterside cafes. It was a nice meal, but one that left me wondering, why did dad think Peter was a skinflint? He certainly had been welcoming and generous with us.

The other experience that still has me wondering, came as a result of our visit to Tanneries du Puy and our meeting with its owner/CEO Maurice Sidem. Of the people I've met in my 37 years in the leather industry, few, if any, matched Maurice's charisma, intelligence and drive. He was a force, in his business, his family and a leader in the French leather industry. The effect he had on the people with whom he interacted was often visceral. People were wary, scared of him. I certainly was.

As I found out five years later, Maurice was not the only person in the Sidem family to be reckoned with. Seasoned by their experiences in the war, he and all but one of his five sisters were strong personalities. They knew how to take care of themselves and the people they loved. And that was what happened to Dad when he met Maurice's sister Paulette, his fashion director at Tanneries du Puy. They met, fell in love, and got married, in 1958, five years after we visited the Sidem tannery. This love story was hard for me to accept when it happened but I better understand and accept it now. Why Dad felt unloved by Mom when he decided to divorce her remains a mystery. But the fact that, in Paulette, he found a woman who loved and took superb care of him when he got sick, is an unquestioned fact. The nine years they had together were happy ones for him and, while I paid a price for his decision to divorce and remarry, I no longer begrudge him his happiness.

There were other experiences, vignettes that added to the texture of our journey. One that comes to mind and gave us fits as we drove from Paris to Le Puy was the difficulty the Hillman Minx had climbing hills. Peter Rabbit would slow down as the grade increased, the engine would sputter and then stop. Then, after 10 to 15 minutes trying to restart the car, the engine would cough into life and we would be on our way. It happened at least three times on this stretch until Pete, our ace driver and mechanic, figured out what might be the problem: vapor lock. The carburetor was overheating. Pete also figured out a temporary solution. If we dampened one of our T-shirts and wrapped it around the carburetor, we might be able to keep it cool enough to keep it running and limit the number of times Peter, the rabbit, decided he needed a rest. The only problem was coming up with cold water. In those days, Chloe was not at my side with the ubiquitous bottle of water she always takes along to keep herself and me hydrated. We had to find some water to wet our t-shirts. So far, we'd seen no gas stations en route to Le Puy. But there was a a stream coursing down the Massif, a hundred feet or so below the spot where Peter Rabbit was having his nap. Problem solved? The cup that once had held the coffee I bought that morning was put to good use. After drawing straws to see who would fetch our water, Ren was dispatched to climb down to get it. When he returned, we wrapped the wet T-shirt around the carburetor. The car started and we took off. Bravo! But the fix was by no means permanent.

The heat from the carburetor would dry out the T-shirt rather quickly, the car would stop and a new ministration would have to be performed. After two or three stops, we were used to the drill. We were no longer worried that we would never make it to a mechanic's shop and get a proper fix. And as luck would have it, the problem was solved during our extended stay in Le Puy, never to return. The delay was annoying but it taught me an important lesson, resourcefulness. In a life that had many hurdles, to clear, I would need to be prepared with alternatives if it looked like Plan A was not working.

Selling Leather in St. Louis – 1955

The next and final semester of Dad's ad hoc training program took place in the summer of 1955. With the two weeks of training in tanning at W. & J. Martin under my belt, the tannery tour of our European suppliers completed and the summer at Phelps Dodge a thing of the past, there was one step that remained for me to take if I wanted to become a leatherman. I needed to get out into the field and meet our customers.

In the years I had worked for dad in the Swamp, I had met some of our most important New York City customers. Sammy Herschkowitz, I. Miller's leather buyer, was a frequent visitor, working with our sorters, "taking over" the leather we would be shipping to him. Sammy and some of the other buyers knew me as a kid. That gave me a head start towards building a trusting relationship with them, but the time had come for me to establish peer-to-peer relationships with all our major customers. As summer approached, Dad had a decision to make. Where should he send me? Which was Loewenstein's most important market? For years, the answer had been New York City. Now, as imports of high-grade women's shoes, first from Italy, then Spain started gaining market share, that landscape was changing. By the time I had finished working at Phelps Dodge, St. Louis had already taken over number one position in terms of sales volume and profitability. Home to major companies like Brown Shoe, International Shoe and a host of smaller ones making less expensive shoes, it was the market of the future. Getting to know the players was essential, clearly something I would have to do eventually. So why not now?

Another factor in Dad's calculus was Herb Bohren, our agent in St. Louis. Herb was a star, a super salesman. He was well respected by everyone, including his competitors, and knew each of his customers intimately. He was tuned in to their likes, dislikes, quirks, strengths and weaknesses. And he had a second sense for when to twist Dad's arm to lower prices or come up with something that would allow him to close on an order. Dad thought he had a lot to teach me. He was right.

And so, shortly after I came home that summer, I took off for St. Louis in my blue VW bug. Where to stay? Having been inducted the previous fall into the Yale chapter of Phi Gamma Delta, residency in the Phi Gam house on the Washington University campus seemed the obvious choice. No problem there, the fraternity house would be open all summer and I was welcome to stay there. The same was true when it came to working out. The free weights and exercise equipment in their fitness room would be at my disposal and with Forest Park minutes away, finding a place to jog safely would not be an issue.

Everything at work also appeared to stand muster. Both Herb and his younger partner, Jim Butler, welcomed me with open arms. A desk had been cleared for me to use at Bohren & Butler's downtown St. Louis office on Olive Street. When we were downtown around lunchtime, Herb, Jim and I would lunch with a bunch of other agents at the nearby Missouri Athletic Club. Those lunches were collegial. Those men, all competitors of ours, would swap stories about the customers they were calling on, a colorful, helpful education for a tenderfoot like me. The same was true when Herb or Jim would have me tag along on one of their calls and introduce me to their customers. Slowly but surely, I met almost all them. There were big shots like John Winfrey, Al Fronciewicz and Willard Schwetman at Brown Shoe, Max Gillette at International, the Lipscomb brothers, John and Mike, at Town and Country, Sam and Billy Wolff at Wolff Bros., Jack Altman at Deb and many, many more. The impression that these men, virtually only men at that time, made on my psyche is remarkable. They were the movers and shakers. They wrote the orders that made our tanning drums hum. Getting them excited about a particular leather was a game I learned and loved to play. Getting their trust and respect became a primary quest and, when I succeeded, my heart hummed along with the drums that were making the leather I sold to them.

That summer was a golden one in my memory of my days as a leatherman wannabe. Besides work, there was also play. Quick lunches at Steak 'n Shake, hamburgers and Coke, served on red plastic trays brought

out to your car by an attractive young lady; feasts at Busch's Grove, re-
plete with a mint julep, a juicy steak, baked potato, and corn on the cob
in gazebos constructed out of 4" diameter, stripped wooden logs. There
were "floats" down the Meramec River with Jim and his family and after-
noons watching him riding his ponies, playing polo with St. Louis' beer
barons and other notables. And there was the occasional date with Mary
John Wilson, daughter of the executive vice president Anheuser-Busch, a
Smithie I'd met in my freshman year who lived on a secluded street near
Forest Park. For a brief while Dad thought she might be quite a catch,
an idea he discarded after I told him I had other ideas that were better.

It was a wonderful summer, but not all of it was golden. One incident
that I love telling people about was my run-in with the St. Louis Police
Department. This caper is not just about me and my naivete. It is about
Herb Bohren and the way he operated. Parking on Olive Street in front
of the B & B office was limited to two hours. That worked for everyone
when we were out most of the day calling on customers. But it did not
work when we were chained to our desks, making calls and dealing with
paperwork, sometimes for four hours at a time. On days like this, getting
parking tickets was always a possibility. Herb and Jim had lived with this
possibility for years and had solved the problem by making an "arrangement" with Red, the cop on the beat. "Stay as long as you want", they
told me. "You won't be bothered." But I was. I started getting tickets, one
after the other. When I reported this to Herb, he smiled, put his hand on
my shoulder and assured me he would ask Red to tear up the tickets I'd
already gotten and make sure I didn't get any more.

Well, I did get more, many more and when I went back to Herb to
find out what he had done with Red he shook his head and said, "I'm
sorry to hear that. I talked to Red about your car before he went on vacation but I guess he didn't tell the person covering for him to give your
Blue VW a pass." . "I'll talk to him as soon as he gets back." Wherever
Red was, he was taking his time coming back. So I kept getting more
tickets. I think I wound up with 15 of them, and one day, when I went
out to get my car and drive it back to Wash U to do my workout, it wasn't
there. Was it stolen? Unlikely, I reasoned. VW bugs were not highly desirable. Next option, could the car have been towed away by the police.?
More likely. Since Herb was not in the office that afternoon, I asked Jim

to drive me down to the station to check if it was there. And, sure enough, that's where it was. And that was the start of an interesting couple of hours. "Oh yes, Mr. Correll, we have your car. We also have a copy of the 15 tickets you've decided not to take care of. With this kind of record, we've decided that we won't let you leave the station, with or without your car, until you post bail." Oops! By then, Jim had come into the station and, after being told bail was needed, he tried to tender the funds needed to spring me. That sounded like a reasonable idea, but one that didn't work. Jim and Herb did not own property in the city of St. Louis. The services of a professional bail bondsman were needed. And that required time – time I spent in a large lockup with a bunch of drunks who had been thrown in there to sober up.

No sweat? Well, not really, except I had been planning to sweat. If this unfortunate detour had not occurred, I would have been heading back to the Phi Gam house and a workout in Forest Park. Instead, here I was, in mixed-up company. Okay, so what next? Well, how much harm would it do to start my exercise routine, right there in front of an audience that would not run for the doors. And so I started, pushups, sit-ups, chin-ups, crunches, planks, the works. All to shouts, "Go man go" and thunderous applause.

After about 45 minutes or so, my savior, the bail bondsman, arrived, plunked down my get out of jail deposit, at last, and I was free to go. The keys to my car were put into my hands along with a form indicating when I should appear in court. Away I went, a scofflaw who had learned a lesson: Don't wait for others to fix your problems, fix them yourself as soon as they occur.

The trial date arrived. I went to court, along with Herb and Jim. Herb, somewhat chastened by the results of his inattention, stepped up to the plate and repaid me the money I had to fork over. Case closed? Not completely. It has one more rather amusing twist. The arresting officer was not Red, Herb's buddy on the SLPD. The policeman who had been festooning my bug with tickets was a drop-dead gorgeous blonde, a rookie Herb had yet to meet and "befriend". And interestingly enough, she did not disappear into the ether of my life. One Sunday evening during TV prime time, I was watching an episode of *What's My Line*, starring amongst others Dorothy Kilgallen and Bennett Cerf. And who to my wondering eyes should appear in front of this panel charged with guessing the profession of the person selected by the show's producers to stump them. You guessed it, but the panel didn't: it was my arresting officer, the lady who caused me to spend a few hours in a lockup in the city of St. Louis. I could not believe my eyes. Small world!

Meeting Customers in New York and New England – 1956

In those days Hermann Loewenstein had a sales office in Boston, staffed with a salaried salesman who called on all of our customers in New England. Manufacturers' representatives, agents who carried other noncompeting leather and findings, sold our leathers for us in the other areas of the U.S. where we had customers. In1956, besides B & B working as agents in St. Louis we had reps stationed in Columbus, OH, Milwaukee WI, Nashville, TN, Dallas, TX, Los Angeles, CA, Lynchburg, VA and Miami, FL.

I'd met a number of our New York customers during my vacation stints as I was growing up. It was time now, Dad felt, for me to renew those acquaintances and to get to know other customers in New York and New England. To help me meet ones located in New York City, Dad had me team up with Charles Recht, his sales manager, Mickey Grossman, a veteran who handled many of our handbag accounts, and Teddy Rice, a promising newcomer, blessed with a streak of Irish blarney. They differed markedly in character and in their approach to making a sale, to fielding a complaint and in befriending the people they called upon. Each man had developed solid relationships with the ones we went to see. My job that summer was to make myself known to these buyers, to take note of their tactics, to decide how to approach them when making a sale and how to handle their complaints. There was more than one way to skin a cat, I decided. And sometimes, I realized, you really needed to be careful, the pussy cat you thought you were calling on could turn into a tiger. And eat you alive.

Besides working in New York that summer, I spent two weeks in New England, working in that office of ours in the leather district, near South Station in Boston. Our salesman up there at the time was an old pro named Al Albuquerque. Loewenstein sold to both men's and women's shoe manufacturers in New England and, in the few weeks I spent with Al, we called on virtually all of them. Al was small in stature and soft spoken. He lacked charisma but he knew his leathers and was well respected. Sadly, I was quick to find out, he also knew his whiskey quite well. Martinis were his favorite libation and rare was the day when he didn't have one for lunch. That didn't seem to bother Al's salesmanship or his driving but it did cut down on the number of customers we saw in a day. Lesson learned for me? Delay your gratification. And I do; no martinis until Chloe and I have our cocktail hour, usually around 5 P.M.

In addition to learning something about salesmanship, I also got modestly acquainted with what our fashion director did when she presented our lines, in our showroom and in our customers' offices. Our fashion director that summer was someone I knew very well, my sister Ruth Helen. Lenie was two years younger than me, a freshman at Brown University in 1955, when Dad asked her to come work for him. She had a flair for fashion, for poetry and prose. She was beautiful, articulate and intelligent, the cream of the crop of the four children in our sibling cluster. Lenie could do anything and everything, a loving sister and friend to me, and the apple of Dad's eye. She was a natural for the job. That's what Dad thought, and when Barbara Trent, his best-ever fashion director gave notice, Dad asked Lenie to pitch in, if only for a while, to help him out. She agreed and for two years did an excellent job working with Dad, building the line and presenting it. She lacked one thing, however, the nerves of steel she would need to fence with the fashionistas at Vogue and Harper's Bazaar.

ACT 4: WELCOME TO THE REAL WORLD

SCENE 1:

Getting Started

I took my first step into the real world of the leather business not more than a week after I graduated from Yale. Taking the old elevator up to the third floor at 26 Ferry St., knowing that a new site on 34th Street between 11th and 12th Avenues had been selected, brought on feelings of nostalgia. This building, Loewenstein's headquarters for 64 years, would soon be razed. I would spend a few short months there before I went off to basic training but, by the time I returned from the Army, it would be gone, history. Dad greeted me as I stepped out of the elevator and invited me into his office. He shook my hand warmly and smiled. His welcome was heartfelt. I could see that in his face. My entry into the firm was the culmination of many years of effort on his part to get me prepared and willing to come work at Loewenstein. He was happy and so was I. Being a leatherman was no longer a stigma. Leather was in my blood and having gotten those job offers from DuPont and P&G, I could hold my head up high. However, his words of welcome, "You can forget what you learned at Yale, you're in the real world now," were ill chosen and not soon forgotten. I bridled. I wanted praise for my years at Yale, not denigration. But now was not the time to discuss how this remark might have hurt me. So, we didn't. We got right down to business.

Dad started off by showing me the drawings of our new office complex. He had once shared with me his wish to be an architect, not a leatherman and his remodeling of our garage in Broadlawn was evidence that this dream to build things was not just a flight of fancy. Now he had another space to configure and he was having a ball. He was pleased with the interior design firm he'd selected and proud of the results they had achieved working together to carve up the new space. The layout they had devised was well done, functional and friendly, a nice place to work and to impress visitors.

The showroom, his pet, was sizable and tastefully decorated. It had a large window on the west wall that looked out on the Hudson River and lit up the room. There was a center island where he would perch his presentations, under which there was space for the horses he would pull out to show off his leather collections. There was room to comfortably seat up to 10 people, a necessity when he put on a show for his shoe-retailer focus groups. Offices for his team of executives were located on this western wall, strung out along a corridor that ran from the showroom to his spacious corner office. Each of the executives' offices had a window, his had two, one looking out on the river. The central office was an open space just outside his door with an entrance to the warehouse at the other end. A small office, with a window looking out on the warehouse, housing inventory control staff, sat just to the left of that door. The warehouse, compared to what the company had on Ferry Street, was gigantic. A counter was being built, lit naturally by windows that extended along the entirety of its western wall. It was there that the rubber hit the road, where leather would be sorted and rolled into bundles and put into cartons to ship out to customers or stored in racks, rows of them, that held the firm's extensive inventory

After helping me visualize where I would be working, he turned to sketching out the plans he had for me. Lying ahead was a six-month stint in the Army. I would have to fulfill that commitment before I came to work full time. My time on active duty would be short, the shortest the Army had to offer, six months, and would be followed by five and a half years' active reserve. When we'd talked years earlier, Dad told me to keep it as short as possible, to enlist in this program rather than the Navy ROTC program available to me at Yale. Joining the Navy, as an officer, had appealed to me. A number of my friends were doing it. Dad was a yachtsman. He loved the sea and may have understood my rationale, but he was insistent; he needed me in the business as soon as possible.

And so, I did as he requested, enlisting in the Army program that required six months of active duty. As I signed up, I was given a date to begin basic training. It would start at Fort Dix in New Jersey in early January the following year. Starting basic training in mid-January meant that I would be back home in August, ready to go on active duty at Hermann Loewenstein by the end of that month. With that schedule in mind, we started scoping out what I would be doing at Loewenstein in the interim, between when Chloe and I came back from our honeymoon and when I took off for the Army. One thing that Dad felt would be worthwhile was for me to work about a month in the A.C. Lawrence calfskin tannery in Peabody, to gain intelligence and build relationships. And so, plans were made for me to do so.

A.C. Lawrence was already Loewenstein's single most important supplier. Our purchases had grown steadily over the four years we'd been doing business. But there was a potential bone of contention of which Dad was clearly aware. ACL manufactured a line of glazed calf quite similar to ours at cheaper prices. Dad and Bill Merchant, the manager of the calfskin division got along well and Dad had an understanding with its sales manager, Dick King, about how we would stay out of each other's hair. Both assured Dad any problems that arose could be solved. But Dad was nervous, understandably so. A.C. Lawrence was a large, multi-plant operation owned by the meatpacking giant, Swift & Company. If push came to shove, there would be little Bill or Dick could do to keep Dad from being edged out. He was right and I was lucky. Things deteriorated, and 15 years later Swift closed that calfskin tannery and sold it to its managers and a group of outside investors. I was one of that group.

With the month of August 1957 now spoken for, we switched our focus to the future. What role did he think I should take on when I returned the following August? Dad spelled out several options and zeroed in on the one he felt might be the best one for me. "How about becoming the sales manager for the J. Mayer & Sohn kidskin line? You've been there. You know their leather and their people. It will be quite a challenge but it should be interesting. Would you be interested?"

I was interested and it didn't take me more than a minute to respond. I accepted his offer, eager to take on the challenge. Growing the sales of this line of leathers would not be easy, but I was game. Walter Schneider and I had bonded. He seemed to understand the U.S. marketplace. I felt we could work well together. The administration at J. Mayer & Sohn was another matter. They seemed set in their ways, but with Walter's help I felt confident we could get what we needed. Going head to head with Shrut & Asch might well be another matter. When women's shoe and handbag customers were looking for color and texture in high quality leathers made out of calfskin, they turned to Dad. In kidskin, they turned to George Shrut. A man with a similar appetite for fashion and aptitude for selling it, George was a force to be reckoned with. As a competitor and, as he later became, a partner and mentor, it was clear I had to be on my toes. I'd have my work cut out for me when I came back from the Army, that's for sure.

With the one-month stint at A.C. Lawrence and my full-time job agreed upon, there was only the time period, September–December, left to discuss. What to do? Dad had some thoughts. I had my own. Preparing for the job I would be coming back to was certainly a priority. Work importing leather from Mayer had already begun, a head-start that I could build on or reshape. Developing peer relationships with our employees was another. I knew almost all of these people and they knew me, as a kid. We talked about each of these options and Dad came up with an unexpected add-on. "I'd like you to take a trip with me to California in early October." He described it to me. It sounded great. And it was – a lesson in how to mix business with pleasure, of how to follow your nose to a great restaurant, a means to bond with a dad not made in the mold of Hollywood perfection.

Having finished our business, we left the office, ready to head uptown, but not before having a celebratory lunch at Sweets. This venerable, unpretentious but world-renowned seafood restaurant was located steps away from our office in the heart of the fish market area along the East River end of Fulton Street. It was one of Dad's absolute favorites. It no longer exists, but just typing its name into my text brings back memories, golden memories, vivid memories, of Dad holding court at a large table, hosting customers, suppliers, employees and family for simple but superlative fish dishes. It was a very special place in his life and mine.

With a good lunch in our bellies, we hiked up to the 7th Avenue subway stop on Fulton Street, took the express train up to 34th Street and hoofed the three long blocks to our new digs at 516 W. 34th St. It was warm that day and we were perspiring as we entered the building, happy to be greeted by a cool interior and an elevator that was a bit speedier than the one we had at 26 Ferry St. As we rode up to our office on the fifth floor, I looked at the list of current tenants. One caught my eye, Coach Leather Goods. It was a small but growing company at the time. Now it's on everyone's lips and on the shoulders of women who can afford to buy their beautiful handbags.

As we reached the fifth floor, Dad's interior designer met us at the elevator and walked us through the space. There were a few details that needed tweaking, but things were coming along nicely. Not much more had to be done and it looked like we would be able to move in, as planned, the first week in August. Dad was pleased. As we walked through the corridor where the executive offices were located, he showed me mine. It was compact but adequate with a window, as advertised, looking out on the Hudson. There was even a desk already in it, and desk chair upholstered in blue nubbly cloth, just the shade a Yale man would want. I was pleased. Finished with our inspection, we walked back to Penn Station. He headed back downtown by subway to pick up his car. I took the LIRR home, to our apartment in Little Neck. It had been a good day.

SCENE 2:

A Trip to California

Our trip to the West Coast began early one morning in September when Dad and I met at Idlewild and boarded a DC-4 to San Francisco. These 42-passenger, four-engine propeller-driven planes were the workhorses of United's fleet at the time. When jets began flying this route the following year, flight time would be cut dramatically. Instead of the 11 hours it would take us to get there, passengers would be whisked to the Bay Area in just over three hours. Today, time seems to be more precious, planes are more crowded and seating is more cramped. Spending those extra hours aboard is something to avoid. But not so for us back then. We looked forward to this flight and the one we would be taking home to New York from Los Angeles aboard a TWA 1649A Constellation. Seats were wide, cushy and comfortable on both of these aircraft models. Leg room was more than ample, the service provided by the attractive, attentive stewardesses hired to see to passenger needs was exceptional, and the food and beverages they served in flight were tasty and free. Even in coach class, which is how we always flew, getting there was half the fun.

We touched down in the in the early evening, rented a car and headed for the city. A light meal had been served prior to landing, but both of us were still a bit hungry when we checked in to our hotel. With the restaurant at the Mark Hopkins Hotel already closed, we were advised we could get sandwiches and drinks from room service. With a busy day ahead of us, that's what we did, then turned in and went to bed to rest up for tomorrow.

In the years Dad worked for Hermann Loewenstein, he took trips – many, many trips. There were always people he wanted to meet, to form relationships that would benefit his business and people, customers and suppliers he needed to see to resolve issues that were best tackled face to face. These were the motivations that caused him to make these journeys, but he would almost always try to weave pleasure into his travels. There would be sights he wanted to see, exhibitions he wanted to attend, friends with whom he wanted to reconnect, shopping he wanted to do and, oh yes, restaurants at which he lusted to eat. I can hear him tell me, almost a tattoo, "Combine business with pleasure" and "Follow your nose when you are looking for a good place to eat."

The trip Dad planned for us contained all these elements. There was a shoe buyer in San Francisco he hoped to befriend. There was a tanner friend in Santa Cruz with whom he wanted to discuss collaborating on a project. There were three customers in LA he planned to call on, one of whom was complaining about the quality of a recent shipment. There was plenty to do when it came to business. There were also plenty of opportunities to have fun. He had been to the West Coast before and fell in love with much that he saw, heard, tasted and smelled. He was eager to share those delights. For me, this trip was more than just that. It was a chance to see Dad in action. It was a chance to step into his real worlds of both business and pleasure. It was a chance to bond, one I hadn't achieved as a child because he was so rarely around when I needed him.

Visiting the I. Magnin department store in San Francisco was the first thing on Dad's to-do list. The manager of its women's shoe salon was known in the trade as a tastemaker. His picks in shoe styles and colors were considered the gold standard by many of his peers. Adding him to the cluster of top shoe retailers Dad convened to preview his leather collections would be a real challenge. But Dad loved challenges. If he succeeded in convincing Mr. X to come, that would be a real coup. I can see us crossing Union Square approaching the building that Christian Dior dubbed the White Marble Palace. I can imagine the adrenalin pumping through Dad's veins and the thoughts racing through his head as he prepared to speak to his prospective focus group member. Did he convince Mr. X to come the following spring to see his fall/winter 1958 collection? I don't know. I was off in the Army when that took place. But I do think he did, based on the celebratory martini we had that night at Top of the Mark at our hotel, staring out across San Francisco Bay at sunset.

The next day we drove across the Golden Gate bridge to Sausalito for lunch. Dad had heard of a small restaurant there, overlooking the bay, that served abalone. Abalone is a mollusk, a marine snail, pinkish ecru in color, that can grow to the size of a squid. It has a consistency of something between a squid and a scallop. It is chewy, delicious and very pricey. Dad had read a positive review about abalone in Gourmet magazine. These delicacies are found on few menus outside of the Bay Area. I can imagine his mouth watering. He was always game to try something new. So, we took the plunge, ordered abalone, prefaced by a glass of California Chardonnay and a dish of guacamole and chips. It was a delightful gastronomic adventure, one wistfully remembered but regrettably never repeated.

After lunch, we headed north to Muir Woods National Park. The grandeur of the giant sequoias that abound there is hard to exaggerate. I was in awe. They are so beautiful, so stately, so old and so tall. They engendered in me a sense of profound peace, perhaps because they have been around so long, able to survive all kinds of wind, weather and man's needs and appetites that have caused other species to vanish. I was humbled then, and I felt the same way when Chloe and I returned with our children many years later. I am not a tree hugger, but I fear for these trees and much else that risks extinction in this world of consumers.

That night's schedule called for dinner in Chinatown and a visit to Ghirardelli Square. I've eaten numerous meals at restaurants in New York's Chinatown, which was only steps away from our offices on Ferry Street. We often offered our out-of-town customers the option of going to a dim sum eatery instead of Sweets. Sitting around a lazy Susan, eating these delightful dumplings and then some spicy Szechuan entrée has always been appealing to me. I won't knock Chinatown in New York, but there is something extra special about Chinatown in San Francisco. It sparkles with lights, sounds and smells. It excites all the senses and when you settle down for a well-prepared meal, you are somewhere close to paradise. From Chinatown we headed off to Ghirardelli Square. The lights, the bustle and the chocolates we bought there are fond memories. Those chocolates are sold around the world now. When I see them on the shelves of a food emporium or pharmacy, conveniently positioned to attract attention, I frequently succumb and buy a box. And as I eat one of those morsels, memories of the times I've been at Ghirardelli float back, tasty memories.

Pleasure took a back seat, so to speak, the next day as we hopped into our rented car and headed off to Santa Cruz to visit the A.K. Salz tannery and meet with its president, Norman Lezin. I'm not sure where Norm and Dad met. It could have been at a Tanners' Council convention or maybe at the Semaine du Cuir or another one of the regional leather shows in the U.S. that took place in those days. It was clear that Norm and Dad liked each other and enjoyed a number of similar interests. The products Norm produced in his tannery, California Saddle Leather, were certainly miles apart from the leathers Dad featured in his collections. But both loved the creativity involved in taking a smelly, slimy, salted hide and turning it into a work of art, a piece of gold. I do think that's the way they thought of what they were doing. In Norm's case, his vegetable-tanned leather found its way not just into saddles. It could be burnished, antiqued, twisted, molded or arranged into works of art. Norm and his wife were starting to collect pieces, some of which he showed us in his office. In Dad's case, it was color, texture and the increasing variety of raw skins he was adding to the mix of leathers he offered to his customers. These were real differences, but they shared one important similarity, the money they earned from selling the products they were making was flowing nicely to the bottom lines of their income statements. There was gold in them thar mills.

I cannot read Dad's mind today, 65 years after we made this trip, but I can guess at what he wished to accomplish during his visit to A.K. Salz. The first thing, I'll hypothesize, was to see Norm's tannery, to get a sense of its operations and a feel for the leather it produced. The next thing, I suppose, was to build his relationship with Norm. Granpere had a knack for building vibrant, trusting relationships and nurturing them. As I watched Dad talking to Norm, I could see that he was good at it too. And the third thing, I have a hunch, was to explore the viability of an idea Dad was working on.

Dad had built a business around calfskin leathers that he sold predominantly to U.S. shoe and handbag customers. He never talked about Loewenstein's vulnerability to major changes that might someday occur in the supply of his raw material or the demand for his finished leather. Why? I sense he also felt, prior to coming into the firm, that these things might happen. I suspect he did not want to scare me off by admitting to those having those thoughts. The difference, I'll hypothesize, is that he felt he could weather the storm, *if* it ever came. Starting in 1953, during the trip he took to Europe with Mom, he began building liaisons with tanners to make leathers for us that would help diversify our current product line and broaden the markets to which we sold them. The range of leathers these tanneries made was extensive, men's weight calfskin, kidskin, reptiles, pigskin, patent side leather, shrunken steer shoulders, and a full range of exotic leathers. Small shipments had already been received from some of these tanneries. Swatch books, product information and skins were being delivered to our agents in the field. Sampling was encouraging, but it would take a while before we could determine whether sales of any of these products, would be significant. In the meantime, Dad had this idea he wanted to explore with Norm.

On one of his walk arounds at the 1956 Semaine du Cuir, Dad had stopped by at a small booth manned by a young Frenchman. Inside that booth he discovered an extensive collection of art and artifacts, all made out of leather. A 24" by 36" framed portrait of a young lady caught his fancy. This unusual work of art was fashioned out of pieces of different colors of suede – pink for the face, brown for the hair, white for her blouse, etc. – had been cut into shapes that resembled those elements, and then pasted onto a canvas stretcher. The effect the artist achieved because of the napped suede he had employed as his medium and the soft colors he had chosen was remarkable. Dad was smitten, déjà vu all over again. He did not pursue this lass as he had Mom, but it gave him an idea. This use of leather was striking, something new, at least for him, got him thinking. Leather can be used decoratively, in art, and not just in paintings like this one, or the collages, veg-tanned statues and other artifacts that were on display in this booth. Why not go big time? Cover whole walls with leather tiles? He could envision all sorts of rooms that could be enlivened or tastefully toned down with artistically fashioned leather tiles. And boy, imagine the size of an order for just one wall of a room!

Dad was hooked. He knew how to antique, burnish and fancy up leather. He'd clicker cut tons of swatches. His presentation skills were up to gaining entry to a totally new market place. There was one thing he didn't have, not yet—a source of vegetable-tanned sole leather thick and rigid enough to be glued to a wall. And that's what Salz made, vegetable-tanned, California Saddle Leather. No, it wasn't exactly traditional sole leather, but if the volume of orders got large enough? Would Norm be able to, would he agree to, making sole leather for Loewenstein? They had become good friends, but would that translate into a working partnership?

Dad had already done a bit of experimenting. He had gotten some sole leather from a friend in England. He had antiqued it in our tannery in Gloversville. We had glazing machines there and our tanner did some trials. He had clicker cut coasters out of the best of the trials. He had started searching for adhesives he could recommend to the designers he would have to convince to use his tiles. He knew that one of his biggest challenges would be breaking in to the world of interior design. He was working on a strategy for getting known, getting accepted and getting orders. That would take a while but, if he could … Norm seemed agreeable to working with Dad, providing him with the leather he needed. Significant expenditures for equipment would have to be made if our tannery was to do the job of finishing, cutting and packaging tile orders. When we left Santa Cruz, it looked like Dad had one part of the puzzle he was working on in place.

The next business Dad had to conduct was two days away, seeing customers in Los Angeles. Our agent there needed to be more active selling our leather and innovative in solving quality complaints such as the one Seymour Fabrik, Vogue Shoe's owner-manager, had called Dad about. In the interim, he wanted to show me the California coast, as he knew and loved it. The first leg he'd planned would take us south from Santa Cruz to San Luis Obispo along U.S. 101. Dad told me I was in for a treat. And boy, was he right!

The Cabrillo Highway, as this scenic route is known, snakes its way south, towards and away from the ocean, all the way to San Luis Obispo, 178 miles of incredible scenery and fascinating history. One of the first landmarks along the way was Castroville, the Artichoke Center of the World. Knowing my love for this veg, Dad decided to take a short detour to show me a field and to buy a couple that we could have with our dinner that night. The next spot of significance, but nothing we cared to or could stop to see, was Fort Ord, a large Army base, open then but closed in 1994. Not far south were Monterey and Carmel, towns much like Great Neck and Manhasset. Dad had visited someone in Carmel on an earlier trip and decided a detour was in order. And so it was, a bit of unexpected nostalgia, as was the fact, unknown to me then, that my friend Dave Strite was in Monterey at the time, in the Army, learning how to speak Russian.

Returning to the highway, now edging toward the coast, we passed over the Bixby Canyon Bridge and, from that point on, until we stopped to eat our picnic lunch at Ragged Point, the Pacific Ocean was right there, over our right shoulders. It's hard to overstate the beauty of this stretch of the Cabrillo Highway. The views were breathtaking, especially at Big Sur, and then, miles later, as we watched the waves crashing into the rocks below and looked back north along the coast from Ragged Point. Sharing this experience with Dad, that was something special.

Just a few miles further on, we stopped in San Simeon to visit Hearst Castle. Dad was eager to show me this historic landmark and had booked tickets in advance for the afternoon tour of the Grand Rooms of the castle. He also wanted to take a walk around the elegant, terraced gardens which parade up the hill from the visitor's center. Since the bus that ferries people from there wasn't in the station, we decided to do a minitour on our own of the pristine and primped lower gardens. The bus arrived and we went up to view the grand rooms in the house. It's hard to adequately describe their opulence. Filled with priceless furniture and artifacts, impeccably chosen and arranged, the splendor of these rooms boggles the mind. As I imagined the Hearst family living in them and the power wielded by William Randolph Hearst in his heyday, I marveled at his ability to build his empire. Today, as I watch cable news, listen to podcasts and realize the effect social media has in shaping today's 24/7 news cycle world, I wonder, what would Hearst's approach be to covering and disseminating the news.

The next day's journey was split into two legs, the first going from San Luis Obispo to Santa Barbara, where we had lunch, the second the stretch from Santa Barbara to LA. The scenery that day was less dramatic, but there was a feature Dad pointed out that I hadn't paid attention to: eucalyptus trees. There were thousands of them, many lining the highway as we approached Santa Barbara. I had never seen a eucalyptus tree before. I remember being unimpressed at first when I did. Their dried out, scruffy look, long, thin silvery trunks, topped with mass of small lime-green leaves were not inspiring. But there was something about the smell of them, "minty, pine-scented, with a touch of honey," according to Google, that somewhat changed my opinion of these ugly spindles. My nose was happy.

Dad was a yachtsman. He'd heard that Santa Barbara was one of the yachting capitals of Southern California. He wanted to see it and show it to me. We had our lunch at Stearns Wharf, one of the many restaurants on the marinas in Santa Barbara. It served good seafood, but the main attraction was being there, overlooking Santa Barbara harbor. It was Sunday. There was plenty of activity on the waterfront. A nice breeze was blowing, and we could see many gorgeous sailboats being readied for an afternoon's sail. We thought about chartering one for the afternoon of sailing, but time would not allow that diversion. Business lay ahead for us in Los Angeles the next day. We had to push on. And so we did, arriving at the Beverly Hilton early enough to take a dip on the pool before dinner.

The next morning our agent, Ernest Kahn, joined us for breakfast. Dad needed to discuss the situation at Vogue Shoe with him. He also was interested in getting a sense of what we might expect in the way of orders from Sobel, Bernstein & Greene and Magdesian Bros. Vogue's clientele included starlets who were fussy and demanding about the garments and shoes they purchased. Color was one of the key factors that determined a purchase and the complaint Seymour Fabrik was making was that the last shipment of T115 Gunmetal Luster Calf was off-shade. Forewarned that this might be the issue, Dad had brought along the color standard our sorters used when receiving shipments from the tannery. Seymour greeted us when we arrived at Vogue and after pleasantries in his office we walked into his warehouse. A bundle from the shipment of T115 we sent to Vogue was unrolled. Our standard was placed on top of one of these skins and, yes, the color was off, slightly darker.

What happened next, how Dad reacted, is what makes this incident memorable to me. Vogue was a good customer, not large but loyal. and Dad did not want to upset Seymour. He did not argue, he apologized that this hadn't been caught before this shipment had been sent. He described two options to rectify the situation. One was to return the entire ship-ment and have it replaced. T115 was one of our most popular shades and there was some in the pipeline. But no stock. "It might take a month to replace his order," he told Seymour. "Could he wait that long?" He asked. The other option he offered was a ten percent discount on the leather Vogue had received. "I know you'll have explaining to do, but do you think that's fair? Would that kind of solution work for you?" he asked Seymour. It would. That problem solved; the rest of the day was spent visiting the two other customers on Dad's list. While no big orders were booked, it was clear that Dad's willingness to fly to the West Coast to visit these customers was appreciated.

The following day, Tuesday, we reverted to tourist mode and had a leisurely day. After breakfast we rode around Beverly Hills occasionally pulling over to the curb to inspect a star's mansion at closer range. Following lunch, we went a step closer to seeing the stars, visiting the MGM lot, a trip to fantasy land, and our final dinner in LA at one of the restaurants patronized by the stars.

Our flight home the next morning was an early one. It had been a good trip, but as we climbed aboard our Constellation, I was looking forward to going home. I wolfed down the light breakfast that was served shortly after take-off, scanned the L.A. Times I'd been given by the stewardess, and then settled back for a nap. A nice snooze was interrupted by an announcement from the flight deck that we would soon be flying over the Grand Canyon. That awakened me. As we soared above this majestic wrinkle in the earth's crust, I sat forward in my seat to see its colors and shapes. And at that point, Dad dropped a bomb. "Son," he said, "I've decided to divorce your mother and remarry." Those words stunned and shut me down, blocking me from hearing words I believe followed, words that must have been as hard for him to say as they were for me to hear. "I've found a woman who understands and loves me, son. I need that kind of a relationship, something that has been missing in our marriage for a long time. Your mother will be hurt, I know that and I'm sorry. I will see to it that she needs not worry about money and she will cope. It will take time, but I know she can. I also regret the turmoil it may cause you, Lenie and Stevie, but you are strong. It is only Judy that I worry about. You are happily married now, to a wonderful woman. She will see you through any rough times ahead. I need the same kind of support and love, son, something your mother has not been capable of giving me. I hope you understand."

On this trip our relationship had just achieved the best of times. He had been around for me in a way I had never felt before. I felt recognized, understood, loved. And now, with his quest for a divorce, I feared we were headed into the worst of times. I didn't tell him that, but no, I didn't understand him. I had no idea of the loneliness he must have been feeling. I was unaware it might have been affecting his health severely enough, my half-sister Suzette has told me, that Dad's doctor advised him to seek a divorce. Could that be true? We were happy, together, weren't we? Perfect people, leading perfect lives? How naïve, how blind I guess I was!

SCENE 3:

A Stint at A.C. Lawrence Calfskin - 1957

Chloe and I were married on July 6, 1957, and directly after returning from our honeymoon in Bermuda, we headed north. A small cottage in nearby Ipswich had been rented for us to stay in while I was working at A.C. Lawrence. Living together prior to getting married was frowned upon in those days and our six weeks living there was a new experience. Chloe and I had known each other for seven years and were very much in love. But as we were about to find out, living together requires an entirely different set of skills. We shared many interests. We were considerate of one another and willing to compromise when our needs and desires did not mesh smoothly. Still, we needed time alone to adjust, and when Chloe's mom came for a short visit, the squeakiness of our bed became a topic of conversation between the two of us. There were other things we laugh at today that weren't so funny then. One was that my wedding ring, a size or so too large, slipped off my finger one afternoon while the two of us were swimming off Crane's Beach. To lose the symbol of our bond so quickly, was that an omen of things to come? Luckily it wasn't.

Another memorable faux pas was taking Chloe out for a sail on the Ipswich River. I've owned a number of boats during my lifetime, starting with the Sunfish we took up to Ipswich that summer. One fine day, I decided to launch it and show Chloe how good a sailor I was. She played along and off we went, but not exactly in the right direction. The breeze was quite strong, blowing from out of the northwest as we pushed off from Crane's Beach. My plan was to tack upriver for a mile or so and then sail downwind back to where we had launched our boat. A short, simple circuit I figured. Unfortunately, it was anything but. The bow of the boat was pointing upriver, and our Sunfish was making its way across the river as planned, but the current was pushing us downriver towards the ocean. The strength of the river current took over. Slowly but surely, we were losing ground. Instead of sailing upriver as planned, we were drifting downriver towards the ocean. Hailing a passing motorboat solved the problem.

We got a tow back to Crane's Beach. I was embarrassed, but we were safe. I realized that I had a lesson to learn, and not just about sailing.

In the years that followed, Chloe and I have sailed on different boats, on different bodies of water and in a variety of weather conditions. There have been times when anticipation of problems that might occur and split-second reactions to counter them were called for. When I didn't need Chloe's help in taking corrective action, I generally reacted, rapidly and effectively. But when I needed to issue her a command to take action, I often was at a loss for words. At times like these, she often told me to "Spit it out." I see her point, but when faced with the need to act quickly to avoid an impending crisis, I often find that taking action myself is easier, quicker and more effective than searching for the right words. As I have learned, as a husband, a parent and a businessman, you need to prepare everyone in advance for what may come your way and then make midcourse corrections as they're called for. Those changes in plan drive Chloe mad sometimes, but this strategy has worked well for me

SCENE 4:

The Army – 1957

And then it was off to the Army, to Ft. Dix. I would be there for eight weeks for basic and then posted elsewhere for another eight of advanced training. Lucky for me, there wasn't much snow in New Jersey in January and February of 1958. Lucky for me that after I slogged through my first four weeks of basic, Chloe was able to come down on weekends. We even managed to have martinis at the rifle range, a pleasant interlude. Lucky for me, as well, Chloe was able to join me for my last four weeks at Fort Jackson where we rented a small apartment off base.

My six months on active duty were up in mid-July. They had been formative but stressful months, so stressful that I completely forgot Chloe's birthday while I was posted at Fort Jackson in Columbia, South Carolina. It was a bone of contention then, when it occurred, one hard for me to live down at the time. But one thing that has marked our 65-year marriage is forgiveness, and she forgave me this faux pas. We can joke about it today though, since we inadvertently organized an indelible reminder that would make it very hard for me to repeat this mistake. A blessing was bestowed on both of us the following year with the birth of our daughter Cathy, born on July 6th, Chloe's birthday. As we drove home from Fort Jackson, I breathed several sighs of relief. I had made it through basic training, I was in the best shape I'd ever been, and I had actually learned something useful, touch typing. My fingers don't always land on the right keys these days, but that training has helped me greatly with projects like this book. As importantly or perhaps more so, I learned a lot about how the other half lives, how fortunate I was and how important it is to build bridges between the haves and the have-nots. The draft, which required me to serve, was not something I looked forward to, but being in military service served me well.

There will be those who disagree, but I feel that requiring young men and women to serve their country is an important formative and unifying experience. As my six-month active-duty hitch ended I reflected on what I had just experienced. There were SNAFUs aplenty in the Army, idiosyncrasies, some unfathomable. But there were also lessons to be learned, important ones, an experience from which I feel young people could profit. Male or female, gay or straight, able or disabled, rich or poor, I think that everyone should experience what it's like to work together for the common good, as equals who rely on one another to get through tough times. It isn't easy and that, exactly, is the point, that we're in it together, no matter where we came from, and we will achieve better outcomes if we join hands.

Our drive back home from Carolina was leisurely. We took a scenic but slower route north, the Blue Ridge Parkway. Wonderful views! We stopped in Lancaster, Pennsylvania, and stayed at Ren's parents' home on Wilson Drive. It felt like old times, being there, seeing Ren, his brother Ned, our financial wizard in later years and their gracious parents, Mr. and Mrs. Z. We also had a chance to have lunch with Chloe's brother Ron and his wife to be, Pat. Ron had a nose similar to Dad's, and he sniffed out a small restaurant in the stockyards where we had lunch. I have an uncanny memory for good meals and that was a good one, a steak sandwich, grilled to perfection, and a heaping portion of French fries and onion rings.

From there we headed for home, a rented apartment, in the same complex in Little Neck where we had lived briefly prior to my going off to basic training. It was good to get back. Things were moving forward slowly as Dad was guided through divorce procedures by his attorney, Lydon Maider. The house in Plandome Manor had not yet been sold, but a developer was looking at it, determining how many lots he could carve out of our three-plus acres. And Mom was sitting tight. All was not totally quiet on the home front, but so far, no major eruptions were occurring in the Correll family.

ACT 5: IN THE REAL WORLD

SCENE 1:

Lectures and Labs in Gloversville - 1958

In the business, there had been a few changes while I was in the Army. Lenie had quit as fashion director, replaced by Rosalind Allen, a vivacious, willowy lady with a fashion flair and a little dog she carried everywhere in her handbag. Another new presence was that young Irishman, Teddy Rice. Teddy was a salesman, personified. His sales pitches were irresistible and when he turned on his Irish blarney, he could chat up and tame even the most grouchy, problematic customer. With Al Albuquerque succumbing, more and more, to his luncheon martinis, it became clear that he would have to be replaced. Teddy was an obvious choice. He had the gift of gab, in spades, and made friends easily. He had been a shoemaker in Ireland, at Churches I believe, but lacked real knowledge of leathermaking. He had to be taught.

And so did I, and my brother Stevie, who seemed destined to join the firm. None of us had been exposed to anything like the program being offered to prospective tanners at the universities in England, France, Italy and Germany. My stints in Glasgow, Offenbach and Peabody had provided me with some of the basics. I knew the mechanics of leathermaking, but Dad felt I needed something more detailed, the chemistry of tanning, to determine if something was going wrong and talk intelligently with the people making our leather about what they were doing to fix the problem. There were always problems that needed to be analyzed and fixed, new products to be ideated and made. He felt I needed that sort of training. The same was true of Stevie. Dad hadn't decided yet what role he wanted Stevie to play in the business. But this kind of knowledge, it couldn't hurt.

While I was away in the Army, Dad asked around about courses in leather tanning and technology. A three-year degree program in Leather

Technology was being offered at the University of Leeds in Great Britain. A friend on staff at the Tanners Council of America had told him about this course and Dad called Douglas Martin to get more details. Yes, it was a good program, Douglas told him, one that Bill Martin, our trainer at W&JM had taken. But three years? Dad needed me now! That's what he'd said to me when I told him that I wanted to enlist in the Army and serve three years on active duty. No, that won't work. How about a plan B, a short course that would prepare Stevie and me to at least talk the talk? Would that work? Is there a professor at Leeds who would be interested in coming over to the States with his family for a three-week vacation on a lake in the Adirondack Mountains? I can easily imagine this sequence of thoughts going through Dad's head. He knew how to get what he wanted!

The answer was yes. A Professor David Tuck was willing to accept Dad's offer to come over, with his family, all expenses paid, plus a generous stipend, to teach a two-week course in the basics of chrome tanning. Super! Having heard a yes, here's how Dad formulated his Plan B. Two cottages were rented on Canada Lake, one for the Tucks, one for me, Chloe, Stevie, Teddy Rice and his family of five; lectures and lab sessions would be held each weekday morning for four hours at our tannery in Gloversville; Saturdays and Sundays would be at leisure for all participants.

And that is what happened. Chloe and I hopped into our Chevrolet Impala on the first Friday in August, drove up to Fulton County and met up with Stevie, Teddy and his gang at our cottage on the south shore of Canada Lake. Professor Tuck and his family arrived shortly thereafter and joined us on our porch for a spaghetti dinner. On Monday, classes began. They were well taught and worthwhile.

SCENE 2:

Earning My Spurs - 1957-1961

As I returned from the Army and started working at Loewenstein, I had more to do than just show I could do the job Dad had offered to me. There were family matters that needed tending to and I felt I needed to pick sides. Supporting Mom who would now be alone seemed obligatory. She would need help adjusting, and I, as her first born son, would now be paterfamilias. Other factors augured otherwise. I would be working for Dad, full time, every day. I blamed Dad for many years for all the calamities that befell Mom and my brother and sisters. But I needed to keep those thoughts to myself while I was at work. And besides, our trip to California made me realize Dad had my back.

Meanwhile Lenie, who was already stressed by her skirmishes at Vogue and Harpers, was now faced with another dilemma, the divorce. Whom should she back? How should she act? She couldn't handle it and went into a tailspin that led from one disaster to another, a brilliant, beautiful girl who wound up leading a troubled, tragic life. And my brother? He got angry, then angrier and left the business after Dad told him he should get a divorce. Dad was right actually. Sylvia was crazy, but Stevie never got over it. He put his energies towards helping Mom, a blessing for her, a blessing for me as I coped with the guilt I felt not rushing to Mom's side. And finally, my youngest sibling, Judy. What happened to her? Judy was 13 years old at the time of the divorce, still a bit young to understand what was going on. Just prior to the divorce, she had been sent away to Stoneleigh-Burnham, a boarding school for girls in Greenfield, Massachusetts. Judy never finished there, and when Mom moved into a small apartment in New York in 1958, after the Plandome Manor property was sold, Judy came to live with her and started her studies at the Art Students League. Her stay with Mom was limited. When Mom bought a home in Manhasset and moved back there, Judy moved in with Dad and his new family.

Judy had talent. Had she not been afflicted with mental illness, I believe she could have made her name in the art world. Her husband,

Leonard, whom she met at the Art Students League, certainly thought so. Sadly, that was not to be. During the nine years between my parents' divorce and Dad's death in 1966, Judy was on the move all over the world and, at least once, in London, I was there to pick up the pieces. That frenetic movement ceased in 1965 when Judy married. But her inner turmoil never ceased and, four years after Dad died, Judy committed suicide.

You get used to things and I did. I had to. I earned my spurs in those early years before

Dad had his first stroke and heart attack. I enjoyed the challenge I was facing. As I saw it, the first thing we had do was to build a market for Mayer's black glazed kid. That was their stock in trade. Dad concurred, but he hoped they would also make a line of aniline kidskin in fashion colors for us. He wanted to have a cheaper alternative to offer to his price-sensitive Technicalf customers. I agreed with him. Having this kind of an arrow in our quiver would be great, a one-two punch. But I knew that it would take more than just gentle persuasion to get what we wanted. Before allocating the time and money needed to develop this product, we would we would need to show the powers that be in Offenbach that we could sell their staple, black glazed kid.

In my grandfather's day, this shiny, smooth leather was his bread and butter. Women's low-heeled comfort shoes, favored by nuns, called "old ladies running boots" in the trade, were made out of it. Small factories in Brooklyn making this kind of footwear were his biggest customers and he sold tons of this kind of leather to them. But those days were gone. By the time Dad took over in 1941, this type of footwear had gone out of fashion, causing many of those factories to close their doors. A change in direction and in products was needed. Dad shifted his focus to fashion, to leather, principally calfskin, in many colors, offered in a variety of tannages and textures. This shift proved successful. Hermann Loewenstein was well respected and profitable on Dad's watch. But we didn't sell black glazed kid or have customers like the ones that bought this product from my grandfather.

Returning to this scenario felt a little like starting at zero. There were still factories making this kind of footwear, but I needed to find them, build relationships with their buyers and prove I could deliver what they wanted, on time. Step one was to start poring through a little maroon handbook published by Footwear News. This little gem, which came out annually, listed, profiled and provided contact information for all the shoe companies doing business in U.S. Thumbing through it, I made note of every company I thought might be making shoes of this kind. Noticing that many of the likely prospects were located east of the Mississippi, I called Teddy Rice, who now covered New England, contacted Jim Butler in St. Louis and talked to Dick Reisenberger, our rep in Ohio, to see what they knew about footwear manufacturers in their areas who were still making this kind of footwear. With that information in hand, I started making plans for trips to call on the companies they felt we should call on.

I enjoy traveling and I love trying to sell something, a product, an idea, myself. That attitude made these initial forays to find new customers fun. I'd learned some important lessons as well during my summer with Herb and Jim in St. Louis and got other insights on how to approach customers during the few weeks I spent with Al Albuquerque in New England. These helped as I walked in to meet buyers we'd never called on. Not every visit was a success, but enough were. The trick was to get someone to place a sample order and then make a cutting test to compare Mayer's kid against the product made by the tannery that was currently his supplier. In enough cases, the results of those cutting tests were favorable and gave us an opportunity to land a more sizable order, say 500 to 1,000 square feet. Then, if we didn't screw up on quality or delivery, we were off to the races, in line to become the company's regular supplier. To me this process became a game that I had fun playing and became rather good at. There were bumps in the road, for sure, like late deliveries and a higher than desirable percent of low grades, which caused some of our cranky buyers to get even crankier. But by and large, our customers were satisfied and so were the powers that be in Offenbach. We were a force to be reckoned with, and they started paying more attention to our requests.

That other wish, Dad's and mine, to develop a line of aniline dyed kidskin for shoe uppers, was less successful. Our dream had been that Mayer could make a product for us that would compete favorably with Shrut & Asch's glazed kid. We got very close, tantalizingly close, but that wish was never fully realized. Mayer did produce an aniline kid lining leather that looked pretty good, and two of our customers tried to cut uppers out of it. Sample shoes were made, followed by a small production run. Things looked promising enough to make us think we had cracked the code. Here was a lining leather good enough to cut into shoe uppers, one that we could sell at dramatically cheaper prices than what Shrut & Asch charged for their aniline kidskin upper leather. If that had worked, we would really have hit the jackpot. But it didn't. The adage "You can't make a silk purse out of a sow's ear" came home to roost. It was a good lesson to learn. Yes, things in the business were going well in those first three years and I was having fun. But there were costs involved.

Besides the guilt I felt keeping my mother at arm's length, I had another twinge of anxiety, fed by my lack of self-confidence. Being heir apparent to my father frightened, rather than emboldened me. What did people think of me? What were they saying behind my back? When they gave me a compliment, could I believe what they were telling me? This paranoia about not being accepted had another wrinkle to it. I was afraid of being completely candid with my fellow employees if I felt they could do a job better. I had yet to learn the difference between criticism and critiques and steered clear of making any comments that might create brushfires in the outback. Lucky for me, I had an ace in the hole. I had a wife who has helped me get through a lifetime of challenges, someone who would nurture me when I was wounded and kick my butt when I played the victim.

Besides the moments of solace and stern reprimand that Chloe gave me, there were two other important lessons I was learning in what had now become my real world. The first was administered by the leather buyer for I. Miller. Sammy Herschkowitz knew his leather. He never missed a trick when it came to finding defects that justified downgrading a skin. He also knew people, and one day he really put me in my place. We had just finished sorting through a pack of leather. He wasn't pleased with the quality of the entire lot and did not want to take it over. I disagreed. "Yes," I agreed. "This wasn't the best load we've ever produced but … it's really not so bad. Don't you agree? Besides," I told him, experimenting with a tactic I watched Dad employ at Vogue Shoe, "it will take a month or more to replace this lot. Can you wait that long, Sammy?" Sammy did not bite when I gave him that option. Instead he bit me. "Rod," he said, "You are a nice guy but you are a lousy liar. Take a look down there at the end of this sorting table. Isn't Joe sorting another pack of this same color?" He was right. Al Tauscher, our head sorter at the time, was just finishing up sorting a load. The skins were being flipped onto the grading horses. Lots of No. 1s and 2s, not many No. 3s. "Why can't I have this pack?" Sammy asked. "No reason," I replied, resolved to forswear fabricating an obvious untruth, at least when dealing with someone like Sammy.

The other lesson was given me by my father. He had just finished a presentation to one of our New York customers. I was sitting in because this firm was buying some of Mayer's kid linings. The showing had gone well. The stylist with whom he was working was impressed, with the leathers, the range of colors and the spiel Dad was giving her about the research he did in Paris prior before making his color decisions. I'd heard him tell our fashion director the sane story, about how he conducted his research, the streets he walked, the show windows he looked at and the shops he walked into to ask a few questions. He was an educated shopper. He knew fashion. He had what he called taste. And he posited that day that maybe I didn't. That caused me to wonder, "If I don't have taste, how can you expect me to run this business? If fashion is its life blood and I don't have taste, what chance do I have to make it successful?"

I felt angry, depressed, hoodwinked into signing up for a job he was now telling me I couldn't handle. That was the message I was getting at the time. But maybe, could it be, that he was telling me something different, something important that would ultimately make me a success? Could he have been saying, "Rod, nobody is perfect and you don't have to be perfect to be a good leader. But you do have to know your strengths and weaknesses. You have what it takes to be a good leader, but taste, in my opinion, is not one of your strong suits. You may want or need to change our way of doing business, but if you intend to sell fashion leathers like I have done, find someone who has taste to do that research for you." I took that advice and like to think this is what he meant to tell me.

SCENE 3:

Running Scared and Running Away – 1962-1965

When dad suffered his stroke and heart attack in September of 1959, it was like someone had taken the air out of a smooth-sailing, high-flying balloon. Dad's personality changed. The business was no longer his priority. He seemed disinterested. He no longer came to the office. He issued no directives to his team, oral or written. The firm was leaderless. In the first four years after this incident, the firm seemed to run on autopilot. The business was still profitable, but sales were slumping and the handwriting was on the wall. High-grade shoe imports from Italy and then Spain were growing yearly. Shoes made by Magli and Ferragamo began to be seen in high-end shoe salons like Saks, Nieman Marcus, Delman. The flood that would soon drown the shoe manufacturing industry in New York and New England had not yet begun, but we were inching ever closer to the tipping point. And when we reached it, all hell broke loose.

Our market, first in New York, then in New England and, to a lesser degree in the Midwest, started collapsing. Shoe imports were rising and nothing could stem the tide. The trend was unmistakable. Something had to be done to adjust to these conditions. Dad still had control. He may have sensed that troubles lay ahead, but he said and did nothing. His executive team, all older and senior to me, were understandably worried. Their jobs were potentially in jeopardy, but with Dad in control, they felt powerless to take any action that might save the day. I was the only family member working in the business at the time, the only person whom, in Dad's absence, they felt they could turn to. Frustrated and afraid, one or more of them would come to me almost daily, requesting that I ask Dad to step down. Questioning Dad about his plans for me was something I'd never done. Confronting him now, asking him to step down? I knew something had to be done to help the business weather the storm, but I didn't have the guts or the heart to tell him to step aside. I couldn't do it. I froze, unwillingly sitting in Dad's chair. It got to the point where I shivered whenever I heard a knock on the door of what was now my office.

I was in a pressure cooker that was not going to stop boiling. I needed to achieve distance, physical and emotional, in order to decompress and clear the cobwebs out of my head. I needed to get unbiased advice, to identify viable alternatives, to come up with a plan and work with it.

It took two years to develop a plan to achieve the distance I needed to start functioning again. With copious amounts of psychotherapy, administered weekly by Dr. Max Brettlar, the family's GP when we were living in Great Neck, I managed to come out of what can best be described as a catatonic state. An escape plan was developed and, with Chloe's support and Dad's approval, activated. It called for a change in venue and my role in the business. Chloe, our 6-year-old daughter Cathy and I would move to Gloversville for two years. I would work in our tannery there, ostensibly as a trainee, getting additional grounding in the art of leathermaking. I would make weekly trips to New York every Thursday, staying overnight with Dad, Paulette and Suzette in their apartment at 24 Central Park South. On Friday I would work in our office, catching up with what was happening and conferring with Dad's executive team. It was a good plan in expected and some unexpected ways. The pressure I'd been feeling was greatly diminished and I was learning more about the dos and don'ts of leathermaking. I was forming solid relationships with people who would play major roles as I rebuilt our business. And perhaps most important, I was seeing Dad in a new light, a gentle man who was there for his new wife and their daughter in a way I'd never experienced when I was growing up.

SCENE 4:

Death and Transfiguration – 1966 and 1967-1971

As the two years we'd agreed upon were coming to a close in mid-1966, I told Dad I wanted to stay in Gloversville. I made what I thought was a good case for extending my stay but he felt otherwise. "We need you back here, in New York," he said emphatically, without spelling out why he felt this was necessary. Did he realize the pressure I was under when he gave his blessing to my escape plan? Did he sense his days were severely numbered when he didn't approve a longer stay in Gloversville and insisted I return to New York? I did not think so then, but I suspect now that he did, agreeing to and orchestrating experiences that he thought would help me step into his shoes.

Dad died on September 12, 1966 of another stroke and heart attack. The need for a reorganization plan was brought to the fore soon thereafter when our bankers at Chase Manhattan visited us. The message was clear: Unless the hemorrhaging of the company's capital could be stanched quickly, my newfound pals at Chase would have no other choice than to pull the six-figure loan they had extended to Dad. I had two years to either increase sales, decrease costs or both. We had made our yearly interest payments on this loan over the last three lean years. It was time now to pay back principal as well.

With that obligation a nonnegotiable fact and the trend of the market becoming clearer by the day, I had my work cut out for me. One of my biggest problems was finding out where to turn for advice. Dad's management team could now look to me as their leader. I sat in Dad's chair and I owned the firm's stock, all of it, Cumulative Preferred, Common B and Common A voting stock. To provide income and ownership to me and my siblings, Dad started making annual gifts of preferred stock. This plan went into effect when I turned fifteen and continued until he had given it all, in equal amounts, to the four of us. Years later, just before his divorce, dad decided to gift all his Common B stock to us. All that remained in his hands at the time of his death was Common A, the voting stock.

So how did I get ownership of all these shares? In a codicil to his will, written only weeks before his death, Dad decreed that my siblings sell their shares, all of them, to me at the book value of our firm at the time of his death. The penalty for not doing so? Relinquishment of other assets he had deeded, in equal amounts, to each of us. The timing of this codicil and why it was written remains a mystery. I was once told that my sister Lenie convinced Dad to write this codicil to allow me to take control, to fight the good fight to save Loewenstein, alone, without the kibitzing that might occur if major decisions were put to four owners, my sibling cluster, rather than just one of us, me.

I now had the power to make changes in direction, in staffing, in allocation of assets, in our business model, in everything. I also had problems, plenty of them. The company had been bleeding cash for over three years. Its net worth was close to zero. I had a customer base that was hurting and shrinking, badly. My product line was predominantly made on calfskin, a raw material that was becoming scarcer and more expensive. And, worst of all, I had three siblings who, under the formula dictated by the codicil in Dad's will, would get virtually nothing for the shares they were being forced to sell me. When I first conceived this part of my memoir, I entitled it "Locked In." That's how I felt. The handwriting was on the wall. Relationships with my brother and two sisters crumbled. Lenie may have understood the future I was facing. Stevie probably did as well. Neither contested Dad's will or the codicil. Judy did hire a lawyer and started to press suit, but not aggressively.

So there I was, the owner/manager of an enterprise that was hurting and needed to be fixed, an asset that was worth close to zero except for one intangible, good will. Over the years, my grandfather and father had built a business that was respected and personal reputations so solid that their word was bankable. They could be trusted to deliver quality merchandise on time at a fair price and, if there were any problems, to rectify them. How about me? I was the new kid on the block. Could they trust me to follow through and behave like Hermann and Rudy? No, I would have to prove myself and, under the conditions I was facing, that would be pretty hard. But I did have a leg up. I had spent most of my life learning how to be a leatherman. I had some knowledge and the start of a track record. It was up to me to find the right goods and deliver them.

Increasing sales is the way I like to make a business profitable, but in the scenario I faced in 1966, cutting costs was the only viable option. There were two major expenses I could cut, the rent expense of our office-warehouse space on West 34th St and the salaries of the people who worked there. The bottom line seemed obvious, I needed to close our New York headquarters, to move it elsewhere and to let people go. As I met with Dad's executive team, I was quite sure what they would recommend. "Stay the course. Give up the space, maybe, but stay in New York. You'll find a way. We'll find a way. But stay." That was also the message of our firm's accountant and a marketing consultant Dad had worked with years ago. Stay, stay, stay! The drumbeat was deafening. I couldn't take it. I called our travel agent, shortly after Dad's funeral, made reservations to spend a week someplace warm, Antigua, packed my bags and ran.

That worked. I got some rest, but not quite the way I had planned. With an immune system taxed by anxiety, I contracted hepatitis A eating an infected lobster, langouste I believe it's called, at our hotel. Hiding from the truth has at times been a survival strategy for me. It's taken the sting out of what I was living through. Hiding from people has been more difficult. Like others in my family, I am plagued by mood swings, sufficient to cause me to be diagnosed as bipolar 11. I have suffered from depressions, never clinical or as severe as those experienced by my two sisters. I have never sought refuge in hospitals or shed unsheddable responsibilities. Not unless I was ill.

And I was ill, quite yellow, with hepatitis A. My doctor told me to stay at home, my wife told me to stay at home, my, yes mine now, executive team said don't dare come in. And I stayed at home. I can't remember any major business decisions I made during this month-long hibernation. But I/we, Chloe and I, made one decision that inalterably changed our lives. After producing a lovely, healthy, intelligent daughter eight years prior, we decided we wanted another child and adopted the first of two other members of our family, our son Douglas. Douglas was a class act and a classy actor, worth another book I hope to write about him and his siblings titled "A Dream Named Douglas". But before that happens, I will write one entitled "Somebody to Love," which talks to the 72-year relationship I've had with my patient, understanding, forgiving wife, Chloe, the story that started me writing, but was temporarily put aside when my relationship with Dad kept creeping into what I was writing. Enough said about the future. Coming back to "Learning to be a Leatherman"…

When I came back to the office, my problems were still there. Nothing had changed. No one had come up with a magic bullet. So, I started to look elsewhere for advice. One source of wisdom was my friend and investment counselor Ned Zimmerman. My account with his firm was minimal when he first started working together. His counsel, while mostly addressed to investment strategies, did not stop there. Ned has common sense; I sometimes do not. He keeps a cool head and measures his response to potential disasters; I tend to be less careful and calculating. Ned helped me frame my problem. Two new friends in Cold Spring Harbor, an accountant and a management consultant, helped me start to put brushstrokes within that frame. The result was an articulated plan, one that I hoped would give Chase Manhattan some peace of mind, to retreat to our tannery in Gloversville, to deal practically and empathically with the employment of the 33 people we had working for us and provide enough cash to start paying back our loan. The plan was accepted but I was not home free. There were goals to set, hurdles to clear and people to befriend and work with. My work was cut out for me when I moved my family to Johnstown and set my reorganization plan in motion. With it, we stopped the flow of red ink, a first step. But others were needed to truly transfigure Hermann Loewenstein Inc into a money-making enterprise. It took two years and a stroke of luck named George Shrut to make that happen. But it did happen and that is a story all its own that's also worth telling.

FINALE:

Epilogue

As you've no doubt noted, my relationship with my father was a prime factor in my struggle to become a man. What may be less evident is how my relationship with my mother colored the way I think, feel, act and react. Those relationships changed rather dramatically as I faced the decision to enter the family business and, even more dramatically, when Dad divorced Mom and married again. Personalities are the base elements of a relationship. Here are my perceptions of those personalities and some questions to which I will probably be seeking answers until the day I die.

Dad was creative, compulsive, competitive, charming, persuasive, persistent and patriarchal. He had vision, taste and a sense of how to spot the next hot fashion trend and respond effectively to it. Most importantly, he had an ability for changing an idea into action. He was a driven man, driven to walk out from under the shadow of his highly successful, admired, well-respected father. And he succeeded, brilliantly, as a businessman. For 16 years, as his father's understudy, Dad learned the ropes, got acquainted with his customers, his suppliers and the agents in the field who sold the firm's leathers. In 1941 when his father died, he took over as its president and turned Hermann Loewenstein Inc. into a fashion house that was the envy of his competitors.

For 19 years, until his first stroke and heart attack dramatically altered his character, Rudy Correll was a major player in the U.S. leather industry. He was a fashion maven who brought color to what had been a rather drab industry. He was an innovator, a developer of a host of fresh concepts and new leathers, many of which he trademarked. Corkette, a shrunken grain nubuck leather was probably his biggest hit, but there were many others. In addition, Dad worked diligently to aid the war effort during World War II. A letter to him from Brigadier General Georges F. Dorict, Quartermaster General, attests to the development of Mukluk, a leather used in boots worn by troops fighting in cold climes.

Politics were not a main interest, but he had his strong opinions and put his money where his mouth was. Last, but by no means least, he was a successful yachtsman, winning numerous trophies while racing his two beloved sailboats, Surabaya and Tomahawk. Long distance races on Long Island Sound became a passion, crowned by the New York Yacht Club sponsored Newport to Bermuda yacht race that he entered in 1957. For Dad, competing against someone was an elixir. On the water, in business and at home, Dad always played to win, and he usually did.

He was less successful as a husband. His marriage started out like something you would only see in the movies. He saw a portrait of my mother on a wall in an artist's studio in Paris, the atelier of a friend of his older sister Elizabeth. He fell in love with that face and told the painter he would like to meet his model. The man obliged, gave him her address in Berlin. Dad got in contact and arranged a meeting on the steps of the Esplanade Hotel, one of Berlin's finest hotels a week later. Dad wasted no time. One date was sufficient due diligence, I guess, and Dad proposed marriage shortly thereafter.

Here the process stalled. Mom's aristocratic German parents, Sophie and Karl Geronne, were not at all sure about welcoming Rudolph Correll Loewenstein into their midst. Dad was not deterred. He called on his father's brother and partner, Wilhelm Loewenstein, to help him out. Uncle Billy traveled annually to Europe on an ocean liner to meet with the firm's suppliers and customers. Accompanying him were his Cadillac and his mistress. He was a supersalesman, an art collector and a bon vivant, well known in Berlin's upper-class social circles. Uncle Billy was happy to be of help and rode to the rescue. Within two months Dad's character was vetted, within six a marriage was agreed upon and an elaborate ceremony in Potsdam was arranged. It looked like a marriage made in heaven. Unfortunately, that's not how it turned out.

Mom was a beauty. It's not hard to imagine what attracted Dad when he saw that portrait of her in Emile Compard's studio. She was refined, well-educated and looked regal in the painting. Equally noticeable was the twinkle in her eye. That must have made him wonder, is she good fun? She came from good stock, he was told. That would be a plus back home. Her parents, it turned out, were prominent members of Berlin society. Her father, Franz Wessel, was one of Berlin's major builders. His wife, Sophie, nee Ingenohl, was a beloved mother and hostess, and Dr. Karl Geronne, who married his best friend Franz's wife after he died at an early age, was pediatrician to Kaiser Wilhelm's children. Her parents were loving, but they were also strict, sufficiently so that Mom itched to get away. The fetters dictated by the culture in which she lived were definitely not to her liking. That itch was bothersome and led her to devise a plan of escape.

Mom had an affinity for language, an asset that she realized might set her free, at least for a little while. By age 17, she spoke three languages, German, French and English, fluently without noticeable accent, took dictation in them and could type letters in all three. She was a marketable commodity, and when a friend of the family decided to open an office in Paris, Mom begged her parents to let her apply for a summer job there. They relented and off she went. Mom never told her kids stories about her childhood. But I find it hard to believe that working as a model for Emile Compard she didn't kick up her heels from time to time.

I can also imagine how this adventurous spirit intrigued Dad and that he wold have done his best to nurture it. It certainly would have been great for my sisters, my brother and me to have that kind of a mom, someone we could play with, someone who would encourage us to be free spirited ourselves, who would offer a shoulder to cry on if we were blue but also be an empathic disciplinarian if we were naughty. That didn't happen. The role she played at home was mostly wife, rarely mother. Looking like she had just stepped out of a Saks Fifth Avenue show window, she would greet guests warmly and see to it that every detail about their meal and their evening was perfectly attended to.

What was lacking for me was emotional contact with Mom. I wanted her hugs. I wanted her to listen to me, to talk to me, to make me feel good, safe and loved. Somehow for her that seemed to be impossible. Why? I still wonder. She was clearly a girl with spunk and joie de vivre when she split from her parents and went to Paris. When did that spirit die? It was not there for us kids when we were growing up. These traits must have been there when Mom and Dad got married, but they were barely noticeable when we were growing up and they evaporated, except occasionally, when she entertained us and our children over predinner cocktails in the home she moved into after the divorce. Tragic.

Why did Mom and Dad grow apart? Why didn't I notice this when it was happening? I've asked myself these questions a thousand times. They had it all. Their health was good, at least until their 60s. They had money, power, friends, playthings and they had us, four sweet, obedient children. What more did they need as individuals, as a couple, as a platform on which they could be the caring parents all four of us desperately needed? It wasn't apparent what was missing in their relationship until Dad filed for divorce. He hungered for intimacy, something he apparently felt Mom could or would no longer give him. But had he, with his need for perfection, crushed her personality and changed her into a mannequin? I suspect that he and his family played a part.

Clothes shopping for her, the interior decorating he took over when we moved to a new home, taking on the maestro roll when events and trips were being planned. Did all these attempts on Dad's part to make everything perfect reduce her confidence? Did they cause her to doubt her ability to skillfully handle these tasks? My guess is yes, they did. But there were a number of other factors that could have precipitated this decline in confidence and intimacy.

One concerns a rumor that Dad's older sister, Elizabeth, told Dad to "ship her back," not long after he brought his bride to live in America. Adding credence to this rumor is news, recently related to me by my half-sister, Suzette, is a conversation that Dad had with "Aunt Betty" early on in his marriage to Mom. In it he reportedly confided in her that he suspected had Mom was having an affair with her gynecologist, the guy who helped deliver me. Supposedly, he admitted that he might have made a mistake marrying her. An oil portrait of Mom, painted two years after I was born depicts a woman who is quite clearly not happy. Her gown is a vibrant red velvet, but her skin is greenish in tinge and her look is distracted and somber. In a recently discovered journal Mom kept around the time it was painted, she muses about walks and a "kissing relationship", she is having with "Uncle Freddy". Portrayed as platonic, this liaison, though clearly restorative, did cause her to question her loyalty to Dad. Could it be that Dad sensed or knew about these walks? Did it cause him to wonder whether the beauty whose portrait he had seen and fallen in love was having an affair? Or was it that she had not passed muster with Dad's family. Dad's mother was bedridden by that time. That his father, never an outgoing personality, affected by his wife's failing health, did not enthusiastically welcome her into the family fold would not surprise me . And his two older sisters, Elizbeth and Marion, both characters out of a dark novel, were certainly not friendly.

A second likely culprit is the presence of Mom's mother, our Omi, who came to live with us in 1938. It was Mom who insisted she come when it became clear that Hitler would soon be waging war. She loved her mom. She wanted her safe, but living together with her under one roof, so soon in her marriage to Dad? It may have been too much for Mom.

Sophie Geronne had been a grande dame, a sought-after hostess in her hometown of Potsdam. She was intelligent, vibrant and personable, fun to be with. As kids, we spent more time with Omi than with Mom. Dad paid deference to her as well and, I suspect, Mom resented that. But because she felt she owed her mother fealty, and perhaps because her relationship with Dad had somehow deteriorated, she said nothing, to Omi or to Dad.

A third stressor, undoubtedly, was loneliness. She was lonely, very lonely. The journal she kept during1938-1939 talks again and again, about missing Dad. He was traveling a lot. He was working hard, trying to measure up to his father. He was crushed when his dad said something he perceived as critical. I can empathize. I felt just the same way, when I started to work for Dad. Trying to please your father, especially when he is also your boss, in the family's business, can be exhausting, depressing and taxing on a marital relationship. Mom writes about how Dad would come home depressed, angry, beaten up, distancing himself from her rather than talking through his despair. I know the scene. I've been there, done that, hiding from problems, afraid to confront them.

And a fourth issue was Dad's physique. He was three inches shorter than Mom and as time went by, his tummy got bigger and bigger. Dad loved to eat good food. He appreciated and relished what he was eating but, unfortunately, he often ate too much and too quickly. I've been there and done that too. I exercise and occasionally fast for a day or two to knock off a few pounds. But I also console myself with comfort food when I'm down and am quick to celebrate a success with food and a cocktail when I have occasion to do so. Just like Dad.

I also share many of his other likes and dislikes. My character traits have been shaped, behaviorally, emotionally and physically by what I saw him do and heard him say, but I never questioned Dad about his philosophy on parenting. With the insights I've gained writing this book, I suspect he'd tell me that experience is the best teacher. I cannot visualize him stepping in to be a mentor as I coped with the learning opportunities, he created for me. But he taught me well, I've come to realize, by providing them to me. I needed those trials by fire in order to survive the challenges that lay ahead, but for years I resented him for orchestrating my existence. As I look back now on the years I spent working at Hermann Loewenstein, I realize how fortunate I was to have been pushed into becoming a leatherman. Blame for the emotional stress I encountered reorganizing the company has been replaced by gratitude. Dad trained me, albeit in absentia, to be a good one. He picked me to address the challenge that was there when he died and he gave me a free, unfettered hand to take it on. If I could turn back time, I'd tell him how well his plan for me worked out and then hand him this letter of thanks and love.

> *Dear Dad,*
>
> *Do you remember I once told you that I wanted to be a teacher and that you replied that teachers were wimps? Well, I took the path you set me on and it worked. It wasn't easy but I was successful. I saw Hermann Loewenstein Inc. through 19 more years, some difficult, some rewarding, before it faced an unclimbable wall and was liquidated. I was the leatherman you wanted me to be. Now I am the teacher I told you I wanted to be. I've taught, in a variety of ways ever since I left the leather business, never in the normal mode of academe, but effectively, so I've been told. I've found that sharing insights and listening to the thoughts of others is a way for people of all ages to learn. The accomplishment I hold most dear is the intimacy Chloe and I have built over the 65 years we have been married. I cherish that union, even more so as we come to the end of our days.*

It wasn't always easy keeping it alive. I've made plenty of mistakes as a husband and as a father. I've found it hard to balance commitments to family and business. It's taken me a long while to realize I did not need to be perfect as a husband, as a father or as a businessman. I've also come to realize that I needn't have feared that your shadow would eclipse mine. I've stepped outside it or embraced it as occasions dictated. It's taken a lifetime. I have finally become my own man, at peace in my own skin. I've been very lucky, Dad, and I owe much of that luck to you.

One thing I did not learn at your knee is the way to build relationships. I observed you in action. Perhaps you thought that was enough. But it wasn't. I could have used your feedback as well when I stumbled. But I made it. I crafted my own way, creating intimacy by letting people feel safe, trusted, listened to. Once I built those relationships, I spent time, loads of time, nurturing those bonds, refreshing them, keeping in constant contact with those people. Doing this has been my greatest accomplishment in life, my greatest joy. I'm glad you too finally found the intimacy you were looking for when you married Paulette and fathered Suzette. But hear this, Dad, please, not as a slap in the face. I had hopes, fervent hopes, when you first broke the news that you were going to divorce and remarry. I wanted desperately for you to change your mind. It is a wish I've carried through most of my lifetime, that you and Mom could have, would have made the effort to reweave the fraying tapestry of your marriage. Time cannot be turned back, but I truly believe had your efforts been successful, that outcomes for many of us could have been better. Mom might have been spared the despair she lived with. The lives of your children, Lenie, Stevie and Judy, lives that were all too short and at times misdirected might have been rerouted, lengthened and made more fulfilling. That didn't happen. It's taken me many years to accept what did happen and to understand

the good that came out of what you did for yourself and for
all the rest of us. You did your best, Dad. You set me on the
right path, with the right tools and then let me find my own
way. I was warmed as I awakened to what you have done
for me and for that, I thank you from the bottom of my heart.
Your loving and grateful son,

Rod

The emotional journey I've taken in writing this book is over. This trip down memory lane has taught me something valuable about myself, about my relationships with people and places, and about events that have shaped me into the man I have become. Today's technology has been an amazing help. Google searches have allowed me to reach back into history to dredge up facts and recapture memories that might otherwise have been unavailable. Emails, Facetime, Zoom and Skype have allowed me a long-distance reach to connect with friends and family to illuminate and add richness to those memories.

Besides the pleasure of reviving these memories and sharing them, an important bottom line has evolved for me. My takeaway is the role my father played in shaping them, a positive one in many instances, I've come to realize. This is quite different from the negative image I've carried with me for many years of the things he said or didn't say, did or didn't do for me. Writing this story has fostered an awareness that brings with it both peace and understanding of how difficult it is for a man to be a father to his children, especially to a son. If nothing else, I realize today, at a deeper, more empathic level, there are more ways than one to be loving and caring as you attempt to prepare your offspring for the life that lies ahead.

Acknowledgements

To my wife, Chloe, my family and friends, Allison Martin Gibbs, Bill Martin and Carol Strite, for providing pictures, documents, missing facts and fact -checking mine. To Alan Lovins, Reed Taylor, Marta Vago and Ned Zimmerman for their careful reading and feedback on what I've written. To Judy Hickey, for her painstaking proofreading. To Wilbur Shapiro, my writer friend here at Avila, for the nudges he has given me to publish a book. To my publisher, Jessika Hazelton, for producing a fine finished product. To my Yale classmate, Peter Wolf for providing me with the inspiration and model I needed to write this memoir. To Rob Brill for helping me find my voice and put readers into the picture. For all the support you've given me in seeing this project across the finish line, I thank you, one and all!

Rod Correll was a leatherman, a third-generation leader of a family business, a founding member and the initial Executive Director of the Family Firm Institute and a consultant to family businesses. In this book, his first, he shares lessons he learned in a multifaceted life. He lives with his wife Chloe at the Avila Retirement Community in Albany, New York.